Ambassadors For Christ

*Sermons Based on Second Lessons for
Lent and Easter*

John B. Jamison

CSS Publishing Company, Inc
Lima, Ohio

Ambassadors For Christ

FIRST EDITION

Copyright © 2020

by CSS Publishing Co., Inc.

Library of Congress Cataloging-in-Publication Data:

Names: Jamison, John B., 1952- author. Title: Ambassadors for Christ : sermons based on second lessons for Lent and Easter / John B. Jamison. Description: First edition. | Lima, Ohio : CSS Publishing Company, Inc., 2020. | Identifiers: LCCN 2020026692 | ISBN 9780788030017 (paperback) | ISBN 9780788030024 (ebook) Subjects: LCSH: Bible. New Testament--Sermons. | Lenten sermons. | Eastertide--Sermons. | Common lectionary (1992) | Church year sermons. Classification: LCC BS2341.55 .J36 2020 | DDC 252/.62--dc23

For more information about CSS Publishing Company resources, visit our website at www. csspub.com, email us at csr@csspub.com, or call (800) 241-4056.

e-book:
ISBN-13: 978-0-7880-3002-4
ISBN-10: 0-7880-3002-7

ISBN-13: 978-0-7880-3001-7
ISBN-10: 0-7880-3001-9

DIGITALLY PRINTED

For those who taught me.

Contents

Introduction

What does it mean to follow Jesus? What does it mean to be the church? Those two questions hounded me as I wrote these sermons for Lent and Eastertide. I have to admit, it was sometimes a difficult journey. Some of the passages here are among those most frequently used to present our answers to those questions. And, those answers we preach are frequently quite different from each other's answers.

We are sometimes a diverse group of followers.

What I offer is my attempt to answer the questions of what it means to follow Jesus and what it means to be the church. I don't claim to have some special insight that makes my answers more correct than anyone else's. But as I get to the end and look back at the words I wrote, I feel they say something that honors the meaning of that amazing experience of Easter morning.

I invite you to read and consider these thoughts and feel free to do what you need to do to make them preachable for yourself. My hope is that, however we come to our answers to those questions, we find ourselves removing more of the barriers that lie between all of us than from creating them.

Preach on!

Ash Wednesday

2 Corinthians 5:20b-6:10

Ambassadors For Christ

He stood quietly and stared out the window. Thoughts were racing through his mind. He paced across the room, then went back to the window. He replayed the memories over and over in his mind. His memories of Corinth. And as he looked out the window he tried to understand what had happened.

Paul had visited Corinth years ago during one of his early trips. It was a busy city even then. Corinth sat on a narrow strip of land separating two seas. Seven hundred years ago they had built a stone road across the land so freight could be more easily moved from ships on one side to the ships on the other. They tried to dig a canal for the ships to travel through more easily, but digging four miles through solid rock was just too much. Periander tried it. Julius Ceasar tried it. Caligula tried it. Nero tried it. The canal would not actually be built until 1893, some 1,800 years later. But with just that stone road, Corinth had become a major city for trade and business, with almost one hundred thousand people living there. But that old city of Corinth was destroyed by the Romans, and the rebuilt Corinth that Paul visited was only about fifty years old. But still, it had quickly once again become a major port, a center for business and trade, filled with people from all corners of the world.

Corinth was what we would call multicultural. It was a mix of Romans, Greeks, Jews, and others, all of whom brought their own customs, languages, and beliefs with them. Corinth was filled with various religious centers, temples, shrines, schools of philosophy, each one presenting its beliefs. And the people of Corinth were educated people. They were familiar with all of the city's philosophies and teachings.

When Paul first visited Corinth, in my mind I imagine he just kind of stood there on a corner for a while, soaking it all in. It was unlike any other place he had visited before. A diverse city, overflowing with beliefs and filled with people who were very serious about the idea of faith. If there was ever a place that he could present Jesus Christ and have a real impact, the city of Corinth was that place.

Paul stayed about a year and a half in Corinth for that first visit. He made his living as a tentmaker, made friends with people like Priscilla and Aquila, and he attended the local synagogue. His message about Jesus did not go well at the synagogue, and Paul made the decision that, from that moment on, he would spend most of his time preaching to the gentiles; all of those Corinthians from the collection of other philosophies and beliefs. They listened to him. When Paul left Corinth at the end of his first visit, he left behind Corinth's first group of Christian believers; he had built a church.

When he left Corinth, Paul knew every person in that church, and they knew him. It felt as much like a family as anything else. As he continued his travels into other cities and countries, whenever he was confronted with difficult times, he thought about Corinth, the people of that church, and he found the strength to continue his work.

As he stared out the window, he thought about those people from that church in Corinth. He was trying to understand what had happened, what had changed, and more importantly, what he was going to do about it.

Paul had just returned from a second visit to the church in Corinth. He had made the trip looking forward to a reunion. He had heard how the church had grown; both in numbers and in its influence in the city, and was eager to celebrate that success with his church family.

But something had changed.

Instead of arriving to enjoy a reunion, he was met with suspicion and accusation. Instead of being welcomed as the one who helped establish the church in Corinth, he was received as someone who was not to be trusted, someone who had presented a false version of the faith, someone who was not to be believed, someone who was not a true disciple of Jesus Christ.

Some of the Corinthians said that Paul was clearly not a true disciple because he did not show his faith through working more wonders. They said that was the true sign of a believer, to perform wondrous miracles like Jesus did. Miracles were important in some of the other groups around Corinth, and as some of those people had joined the church they brought that belief with them. Jesus did miracles, so it was perfectly obvious to them that if Jesus was really with them, then his followers would be able to be miracle workers as well. "If you were a true disciple, then show us your miracles."

Another group of church members had been impressed by the style of some of the other traveling preachers that had come to town since Paul's last visit. These preachers were far more articulate than Paul. They did not just talk like Paul talked; they spoke in a way that said as much to the eyes as it did to the ears. They were practiced and polished, and very clear about who the enemies were. They sounded the way you would expect someone speaking for God to sound. They dressed that way too. While Paul wore simple clothes, these new preachers wore the best sandals, the best robes, and had their hair done at the very best of the city's salons. These preachers demonstrated the presence of someone that God had selected to truly lead the church, to offer them something that Paul was clearly not capable of. I mean, just look at him. Just listen to him. And anyway, what miracles had he performed?

The visit had very quickly become difficult. There were those in the church who still believed in Paul, mostly those who had been there since the beginning. The groups began to argue. Even if Paul did have the things to say to calm the storm, he was out-talked by the practiced and polished preachers; this is the kind of confrontation they were well prepared to handle. They easily reinforced their argument that Paul was not the voice of Jesus Christ, but was just another of the enemy they all knew was out to get them.

Paul did the only thing he believed was right. He left.

The practiced and polished preachers celebrated their victory over the enemy. The miracle-worker preachers celebrated how God had worked yet another wonder and driven away the false prophet.

Paul stood quietly and stared out the window, thinking about how the group of people that had begun as a movement of faith, hope, and openness had become a place of division and disappointment.

I have an idea that some of us may have stood quietly, staring out that window, trying to understand what had happened. I have stood there. There have been times when I have been faced with experiences in the church that seemed so far from what I thought the church was when I first came to it. There have been times in my own personal faith when I felt and experienced things that seemed so far from what I felt and experienced in those first days of my faith. I have stood at the window trying to figure out what happened. What changed? Was my first experience wrong? Did I misunderstand something and am just now seeing the truth? Or has everything else gone wrong and I'm the only one who has this faith thing actually figured out? Just what the heck is going on here?

I have tried to figure out what to do about it. Should I stand up and confront someone, and just let the results happen? Should I be angry, sad, or just shrug and walk away? Is my faith today, and my church today, being driven by the same things it was when it was first so real to me? Or has it become distracted by something else; fancy words and appearances, or expectations and rules that someone added? Am I living my faith, or have I somehow gotten distracted? As a person of faith, what am I to be? As a church of faith, what are we to be?

These are good questions to ask on Ash Wednesday. The idea of Lent is to spend the next seven weeks preparing ourselves for what happens on Easter Sunday. Whatever else we might do this Lenten season, why don't we spend some time asking ourselves those questions once again?

For today, let's look at what Paul found as his answer, and how he responded to the church at Corinth and others after.

Paul had choices. He wasn't a practiced and polished speaker, but he could write. He could write a scathing letter to the Corinth church, attacking his attackers and trying to encourage his loyal followers to fight the good fight. Or, he could just go back out on the road and leave the Corinth church to its own mess. It would serve them right. Paul decided to write, but not a scathing attack letter that would just stir things up all that much more. Let's look at what he did write.

In the chapter right before our reading, Paul reminded the Corinth church of the core reason they were created in the first place by saying that anyone who is with Christ is part of a new creation; one that no longer regards anyone from the old human point of view. Rather than try to argue with the polished and practiced preachers or the miracle workers, he simply said that those things we used to use to evaluate people just didn't count anymore. Looking and sounding fancy, being able to do fancy things just didn't matter. Those were not the signs of someone who was a disciple of Jesus Christ.

Paul wrote that the true disciple, fancy or not, is the one who lives their life as Christ's ambassador — the one who represents Jesus — who does what Jesus would do. He didn't just leave it open for them to argue about what it meant to do that. He gave them a list of things that described the work of a true ambassador of Jesus Christ. It said nothing about fancy clothes or fancy talk, and it said nothing about miracles. Paul wrote that those living the faith of Jesus Christ are:

Treated as imposters, and yet they are true.
[Treated] as unknown, yet they are well known.
[Treated] as dying, yet they are alive.
[Treated] as punished, yet they are not killed.
[Treated] as sorrowful, yet they are always rejoicing.
[Treated] as poor, yet they are making many rich.
[Treated] as having nothing, yet they possess everything.
(2 Corinthians 6:8-10)

It reminds me of that day the followers of John the Baptist asked Jesus if he was really the one they had been waiting for. Jesus didn't quote scripture about prophecy or get all theological. He simply told them to take a few minutes and look at what he and his disciples were doing there and see what they thought. They looked at the impact Jesus and his disciples were having and they went back to John and said, "Yep, he's the guy." Paul's idea was that an ambassador of Christ would

13

have the same impact.

As we go through this Lenten season, let's take a look at Paul's job description for an ambassador of Christ, and let's just see how we're doing; individually and as a church. Let's see what we find as we think about our role as people of faith, not by a collection of rules to follow, or enemies to do battle with, and not even about how our faith impacts our own lives; if it makes us feel better, or safer, or more successful, or more right. But let's look at how we treat others, and the impact our lives of faith is having on others, those around us, whoever they might be. How are we doing with the whole idea that, as people of faith, we no longer regard any people from the old human point of view; any people — any people at all?

Easter is coming. We have been appointed as ambassadors of Christ. Let's take some time and get our resumes in order.

Amen.

First Sunday in Lent

1 Peter 3:18-22

A Letter In Time

Let's just be honest about it. What we are all trying to do here is difficult. We can pretend it isn't. We can pretend that it gets easier. We could stand here and say, "If you just try harder, and believe more, the bad stuff will all go away and the really good stuff will start to happen. It will all get easier if you just believe." The problem with that is that, for a lot of us, we spend most of our time wondering, "Okay, just when is that going to happen? How much harder do I have to try? How much more do I need to believe? I thought I was doing that… but, it sure doesn't feel like it's getting any easier. Just when does it get better?"

For some of us, it takes until we finally get tired of trying harder, and we find it more and more difficult to believe in much of anything. We just settle. We settle for surviving; for getting by. Our life of faith becomes a way to just get us through the day. Some of us come here on this first Sunday in Lent because it is a part of our settlement; something we do to get enough "juice" to hopefully keep us going until another refill next week. Our faith is important to us. But it isn't really what we expected back when we started this whole life-of-faith thing.

So, let's just be honest about it. Being an ambassador for Christ is difficult. That's how Paul described our job as people of faith; to be Christ's ambassador. On our own and as a church, we are to represent him in our world; to live our lives the way we believe he would live his life, here and now, in this time, in this place. When people encounter us, they encounter Jesus. When we come into someone's life, it's like Jesus came in. At the end of the day, when we look back at all of the steps we took during that day, it looks like Jesus had made those steps.

Sounds a bit wild and overly dramatic? Yeah, it really does, doesn't it? Some of you are rolling your eyes just a bit, settling back in your seat while the preacher gets all theological on you for a while. Seriously, to think that we might be expected to actually our lives the way Jesus would live his life is a bit much, isn't it? I mean, after all, he was the Son of God. He had some special insight or something, didn't he? And what am I? I'm just, I'm just me.

I'm supposed to live like Jesus? Just what does that actually mean anyway? You're going to say that if I really want things to get easier and better; if I really want to be happy and successful, I need to do what? I need to go off and join some group in the wilderness somewhere, give away all of my stuff, or memorize a bunch of scriptures and follow a bunch of rules? Just what does it mean to be Christ's ambassador? What does it mean to live my life like Jesus would live his so everything will get easier and better?

Over the next few weeks, as we get ready for Easter Sunday, we're going to try and figure that out. We're going to try and understand, for each of us in our own lives, and all of us together as a church, what it means to be Christ's ambassador; right here and now, in this time, in this place. Today, we're going to see what we might learn from that passage in 1 Peter. But as we get started, I need to take a few minutes to be very clear about what Paul meant when he called us ambassadors because it's a bit different from what we might think about that role.

We might think about an ambassador as a person living in one country as the representative of another country. They have a key role in politics and leadership. They live in an embassy, with guards to protect them, and they have special rewards and privileges that come with the role. That's not what Paul was talking about. Christ's ambassador has the same protection, rewards, and privileges that Jesus had, and that means they don't have any. They have no special rewards or privileges. They are not going to live in a secure embassy. They are vulnerable. They are going to suffer.

Let's just be honest about it. What we are all trying to do here is difficult.

Jesus never tried to make things safer, easier, or better for himself. He spent his time doing whatever he could to make life better for those around him. Jesus did not go through the day following or enforcing a long list of rules and laws. He spent his time touching those people the law said were untouchable, eating dinner with those the law said were unclean, and giving hope to those the law said were beyond hope. And he paid the price for what he did. And that is our job description as Christ's ambassador. Easier and better is not a part of the deal.

But wait. Doesn't it say somewhere that if we ask, we will receive, and if we seek, we will find? What about that? Doesn't that mean things can get better if we believe and ask for things to make it better?

The simple fact is that an ambassador for Christ is going to ask for different things than someone living some other kind of life. Christ's ambassador is going to ask for and seek for the things that Jesus himself would ask and seek for; things that will make a difference in the lives of others, not his own. So, yes, faith does bring results now, but not the kind of results we might be thinking about. What we are all trying to do here is difficult.

That brings us to the passage from 1 Peter, although we might be wondering what that talk about Noah has to do with us living our lives the same way Jesus lived his. Noah? And that part about only eight people being saved? What is that all about?

It might help to understand why this letter was written in the first place, and to whom it was written to. If we want to understand what was written in the letters of the New Testament, we need to understand who they were written to and why they were written. The books like 1 Peter weren't intended to be made a part of a bigger book and be passed down through history so you and I could read them here today. They were letters, written to a specific group of people, about a specific thing, to help them understand what they should do about that thing. So if we don't know who it was written to, or what the thing was that they were dealing with, it's pretty hard to understand what the person writing the letter was actually saying.

Before anyone squirms too much, understanding that reality does not weaken the scriptures, and it does not make them any less meaningful. In fact, it is kind of exciting to think that we might actually be understanding the scripture a bit better when we understand what they were really talking about. Let's try it with today's passage.

First of all, it will help to know that the letter was written sometime near the end of the first century, to a group of people who were getting a lot of pressure for becoming Christians. There didn't seem to be any formal, government pressure against Christians yet, but the problems were with the rest of the community. Becoming a Christian was not an acceptable thing to do. Many of the people in the church had once been active and important members of the community. But when they became Christian, the community turned against them and no longer associated with them. They were no longer welcome in the community. Because of their beliefs, the Christians disagreed with many of the things the community was doing and disagreed with many of the institutions of the community. The Christians were seen as dangerous, as members of a group that was out to destroy the community and what it stood for. Because of the pressures, some church members ended up leaving the church, some decided to stand up and fight, while others decided it was much easier to leave the community completely.

Relationships were destroyed. If a husband or a wife converted and the other spouse did not, they either fought or one left. If a slave converted and the owner did not, the slave was either severely punished or ran away. Instead of representing that source of healing and unity that Jesus had lived his life to be, the church had become something that was causing the community to destroy itself. The letter we are reading today was written to the members of that church, in that community, about that problem.

The letter was written to gentiles and former Jews who had converted to become a part of the church. The story of Noah was certainly well known to the former Jews and was a story that even the gentiles would have been familiar with. Talking about Noah helped them all understand that Jesus was associated with that old tradition and that powerful God from the old scriptures.

Jesus was not only related to that old tradition, but think about it: If you think Noah's miracle was something, Noah's big boat only ended up saving eight people. Jesus saved everyone! Listen up people, what Peter is writing about in this letter is pretty big stuff. You have made the right choice by following Jesus, even if that meant having to suffer through the things the community was doing to them.

That was the message of the letter.

What they were all trying to do there was difficult. Instead of having things easier and better right now, they would suffer because of what they were doing. Jesus suffered and did not quit, and anyone representing Jesus faced the same thing. An ambassador will not fight back and an ambassador will not run away.

That's what the letter was about. An ambassador of Christ will stay and suffer willingly to set an example for the way things should be done, the way Jesus lived his life.

That may help us understand some of the other things the writer of this letter said as well. Some of them seem pretty hard to understand otherwise. For example, in chapter two, the writer said Christians should accept the authority of every human institution, even when those institutions do evil things. And he said that slaves should accept the authority of their masters. In chapter three, the writer said that wives should accept the authority of their husbands, even when they are not obeying God's word. And he wrote that husbands should show consideration for their wives and honor them, even though they are the weaker sex.

You have heard those words before and it is very possible that, sometimes, you may have heard those words being used to say things the writer of 1 Peter never intended them to say.

I have heard people say that these words mean that marriage is not a relationship of equal partners, and that wives should unquestionably obey their husbands because the Bible says that women are somehow less than men. I have heard people say that these words mean that the practice of slavery is something that is biblical and something of which God approves. I have heard people say that these words mean that we should obey the authority of anyone in a position of leadership, even when that leadership is cruel and ungodly. But if we read the words of 1 Peter as they were written to this specific group of people, in this specific place and time, with their specific issues, I believe we find that those written words may be saying something very different.

The writer of 1 Peter did not condone slavery, women being second class citizens, or leaders doing a poor job of leading. Good or bad, right or wrong, those were issues of the human world, and the writer was writing about that world. The letter was not written to address the issues of equal rights, slavery, or socio-political issues relating to any government leadership. It isn't that those are not important issues but the letter was written to address the very simple question of what an ambassador of Christ is to do when they are caused to suffer because of their faith. The writer was not writing to be quoted by those who believe that women are less than men, that owning slaves is fine, or that leaders should be obeyed no matter what. He was writing to remind a group of Christian that Jesus Christ presented a very different world and that the role of Christ's ambassador was to set the example of what that new world was about, to try and convert others to join them in that new world. He was writing to say that if you suffer because you choose to follow Jesus Christ, you are to accept that suffering as Jesus accepted his suffering, and set an example of what it means to be a follower of Jesus Christ.

I need to add one more thing. You may have heard people quote the words of this letter to say that a wife should accept the authority of her husband even if that husband acts in ways that are fully abusive, physically or mentally. You may have actually heard abused women be told that they need to return home, to face more abuse, because the Bible says they are to honor and obey. Be very clear. That is not what the writer of 1 Peter was writing. There is a very real difference between being treated differently because of our faith and being abused because someone is out of control. Jesus lived his life to free the abused from their abusers, and an ambassador of Christ will do the same.

Again, what we are all trying to do here is difficult. When things get difficult, it is much easier to get all wired up and fight, to look for ways to attack and somehow weaken the power of those making us suffer. It is much easier to separate ourselves from those people and their world, to label it as evil, and to spend our time with those people who see things our way. We are not to use our faith as an excuse to run, or fight, or do things that will serve to destroy and do harm. Following Christ is never a promise of a good time but is an acceptance of the reality of living life differently.

But before we stop, let's be honest again. Promising some way to avoid suffering and make life easier is something that makes this 'being a Christian" thing sound a lot better on a banner. I mean, let's be real here. The idea of willingly accepting suffering sounds pretty dumb. If we are going to be punished because we follow Christ, why would anyone want to follow him? Paul even wrote to the church in Corinth saying that we may be punished, but we are not killed.

That makes a pretty poor sales pitch.

The true role of Christ's ambassador is a very different role, based on a very different promise. It is a role that seeks to remove the suffering of those around us and sees our own suffering as one of the ways we make that happen. We don't need to fight it or run from it, and we absolutely do not see our suffering as an indication that our faith is weak. It is a sign that we are trying to be different. It is a sign that we are trying to live our lives as we are called to live them; as ambassadors for Jesus Christ.

Amen.

Second Sunday in Lent

Romans 4:13-25

Knowing, And Known

He leaned back against the tree and watched the crowds move past. They all looked so young. He smiled a bit as he thought about how young he had been that first time he brought his flocks here to sell. That had been, what, seventy years ago? Maybe eighty? The journey from home to the market hadn't changed any, but it sure felt like it had. He couldn't remember ever feeling this tired. He looked down at his campfire and wondered if this would be his last trip; the last time he would make the long journey to bring his flocks and sit under the big oak tree.

When he looked up, he noticed the three men slowly walking past. Although they were younger than him, they looked about as tired as he felt. He raised his arm and waved them over. The three men nodded, put down their heavy bags, and sat on the ground next to the fire. Without speaking, the old man stirred the embers to bring the fire to life. He filled the small pot with water, ground a handful of leaves and when the water began to steam, he dropped them in the pot. The old man got four small cups and set them on the ground in front of him. When he decided it was ready, he lifted the pot and slowly filled three cups with fresh, warm tea. He lifted one cup and held it out to offer to one of the visitors. The visitor shook his head and held his hands up to say no to the tea. The old man offered the cup a second time and the visitor again refused to accept it. A third time the old man held out the cup. The visitor smiled, nodded his head, and took the cup. The same thing was done for the other two visitors until finally, all three accepted their tea and the old man poured the fourth cup for himself.

When the cups were empty, the old man told a servant to prepare some fresh steaks for the guests, and the old man's wife started baking some bread, all to make the visitors feel welcomed.

Then they began to speak.

I don't know what all they talked about, but the old man did his best to make the visitors feel welcome. He offered them the hospitality that a bedouin (nomad of the desert) was taught to offer. The desert could be a dangerous place. There were no fast-food stops, no gas stations, no discount stores to run in and buy water at. A bedouin knew very well that if they were ever caught out on their own, away from their tent and supplies, they could not survive for long. If a bedouin saw someone in that situation, it was their responsibility to see that the traveler was offered food and shelter. It was difficult sometimes when the traveler and the bedouin did not speak the same language. That's the reason they started with the tea.

The tea established the agreement between the host and the guest, even if they could not speak. A cup of tea was offered to the guest, and they refused. It was offered a second time and refused. It was offered a third time and accepted. It was a simple way of saying that both parties understand that the visitor is welcome as a guest, to eat and sleep in the safety of the bedouin's home. But on the third day, they have to leave.

It was an old tradition and, unfortunately, it was one that was not practiced that much anymore. By the time the three men approached the old man's tent, they had already passed a dozen others that did not wave or offer a cup. That was one of the things that may have impressed the visitors. We don't know how long they actually stayed with the old man; if they stayed the three days or just finished their tea and conversation and went on their way. All we know is that as they prepared to leave, the visitors asked the old man about his family. He explained that it was just him and his wife. He said they although they had always held out hope, they had never been blessed with children. He said that it had been a disappointment, especially to his wife, but now that they were as old as they were they just accepted it and were thankful for what they did have.

The three visitors paused. Then one asked the old man where his wife was. He said, "She's in the tent." I think he kind of smiled as he said it, knowing full well that she was probably standing just inside the flap listening to everything they had been saying. The visitor smiled, and said, "I'll tell you what. We will come back and see you here at next year's market and we'll enjoy saying hello to your new son, too." (Genesis 18:2-15)

I have to say that this next part is not in the passage, but I'm betting it happened just the same. It started in one of those little lines near the corner of her mouth; one of those lines that showed up several years ago. That line kind of curled up, followed by several of the other lines around the wife's mouth and cheeks, until her face had pulled itself into a full-blown grin. Then the grin turned into a laugh. The visitor smiled again and said that they might laugh about the idea of having a son right now, but hang on. If God said you were going to have a son, do you really think something like your age was going to stop it? The visitors left.

It was a story Paul knew they would all remember. Paul was writing to people in Rome, to the new Christian community and the Jewish community who were in a real mess. There had been the same ongoing conflict between the Jews and the new Christian community that had happened in other places. But the situation in Rome had become even more destructive. The Roman leader, Claudius, had branded the Jews as enemies and expelled them from Rome. However, Claudius did not consider the new Christan group to be big enough to be a threat, so they were allowed to stay. For a while, that ongoing struggle between Christians and Jews was gone. Then, Nero took charge and removed the ban, allowing the Jewish community to begin returning to the city. And now, instead of the older Jewish community being the established group, the Christians had taken that role. The returning Jews were the newcomers trying to reestablish themselves. The division between Christians and Jews was now greater than ever, and Paul was writing to try and bring that to an end.

Paul's background gave him an advantage. He had grown up as a Jew. He was raised in a well-established family with the right lineage. He studied under the best teacher in Jerusalem and learned the Jewish laws from front to back. He became a member of the Pharisees, the group responsible for enforcing and protecting those laws. So he understood what it meant to be a faithful Jew. He had been trained to live it.

Then he converted and became a Christian. He became as serious about his new faith as he had been about his old. He traveled the world, preaching about Jesus and helping create churches. He understood what it meant to be a faithful Christian. He was trying to live it now.

But, Paul's background also gave him a disadvantage. For the Jewish community, having someone in such a significant role as Paul not only walk away from the faith but take such an active role against the faith was simply unacceptable. It was one thing for some gentile to join the Christians, but Paul? It was far too dangerous and set far too dangerous an example. It was simply unacceptable.

As Paul preached about Jesus Christ, those hearing him sometimes wondered if this man, who had once been a Pharisee running around arresting and helping kill Christians, could really be trusted. Or, was this conversion thing just another very smart way of getting inside to set the trap for more? Even as he suffered for his work serving Jesus Christ, there were many who questioned who he was really working for.

Paul had other disadvantages with the Christian community, many of whom were former Jews who had converted as he had done. But though they converted, they still held tightly to some of the pieces of their Jewish faith. It was not just the belief of those Christians still in the area around Jerusalem. As Paul traveled, he frequently found people who believed in Jesus Christ, but they also believed in some of the old laws from days past. Laws like men of faith needing to be circumcised, those that defined what you could and could not eat, and who you could or could not eat with. Those were just a part of the lifestyle of Jews who became Christian, and they held on to them. It was a simple belief that the person known as true Christian will obey those laws.

But gentiles had not lived with those old laws, and to be honest, most were not all that excited about the idea of circumcision or giving up some of their favorite foods and friends just because of an old Jewish law. As they saw it, they weren't becoming Jewish, they were becoming Christian. For them, there was a difference. The true Christian is not known by those old laws.

While the gentile church refused to follow the old laws, the others refused to recognize anyone as Christian who did not comply with those laws. Paul stood on the side of the gentiles, which earned him points with them, and cost him points with the rest.

And, just to complicate things a bit more, Paul still tried to support the home church in Jerusalem by collecting money during his journeys and sending it to Jerusalem. Even then, each time he went to Jerusalem to deliver the gift, someone either in the Jewish leadership or the Christian leadership tried to find a way to arrest him.

Paul believed this division had to be dealt with, so he wrote a letter to the people all caught up in the fighting in Rome.

Those were the people Paul was writing to in today's scripture, and that was the situation they were in that he was writing about. Not only was there a division between Christian and Jew, but there was also division between gentile Christian and Jewish Christian. Paul wrote to try and change that.

He saw three major issues. First, the argument between the Christians themselves about following the old laws. Second, the basic difference between the Jewish faith and the Christian faith. Third, was the way the Christians were mistreating the Jews who were returning to Rome.

There have been a lot of sermons preached and a lot of books written to explain what Paul said in the letter to the Romans, but let's see if we can understand enough to help us think about it all today. Paul actually makes that kind of easy if we take a quick look at the first few chapters.

In the first chapter, after the usual greeting, Paul began by reminding the readers that no one of them is perfect and free from sin. He wrote that even though they know what God does not want them to do, they not only keep on doing those things but approve when those things are done. Romans.

In chapter two, he wrote that since they all fall short, none of them had any excuse for passing judgment on anyone else. (Romans 2:1) They were in the same boat one way or the other. If it's not circumcision or food, it's something else. As far as God was concerned there was no division between them. None of them were in a position to evaluate others or see themselves as more worthy than anyone else.

Then Paul went to the core issue of knowing what it meant to be Christian, what was required to live as a follower of Jesus Christ. He started by admitting that there were advantages to being a Jew because they were already familiar with the old stories about God and how that faith had come to be. But, he then added, that did not make them more righteous or holy, and in fact, they had misunderstood those stories anyway.

He talked about the old man sitting outside of his tent; the man whose name was Abraham, with his wife Sarah. Abraham's visit with the three strangers was seen as a starting point for the faith; the day God selected Abraham to be the father of nations (Romans 4:19). There was no greater honor than to be able to trace your family lineage back to Father Abraham. It was a story that started the journey to Moses, to David, and for the Christians, to Jesus himself. All of his readers, regardless of which side of the fight they were on, knew about Abraham. When Paul said they had the story wrong, he had their attention.

Paul's argument was simple. Did Abraham and Sarah have the baby Isaac because they followed the laws of Moses or because they had faith that God's word could be trusted? The answer wasn't that difficult since Moses wasn't even around yet when Abraham met the three guys, but to help them along Paul then wrote the passage from Genesis that said,

"Abram believed the Lord, and he credited it to him as righteousness."

(Genesis 48:6)

Abraham was not righteous because he followed a law, was circumcised, ate the right foods, ate with the right people, because of or any of the other laws that filled the books in the Pharisee's library. Abraham believed, and he was known as righteous. If you want to know you are a Christian, believe in Jesus Christ.

Paul wrote a lot more in the letter to encourage the people in Rome and to help them make the adjustment to a new way of thinking, but I think we have heard the message he had in mind for them. It's a message that might be worth thinking about as we go through Lent asking what it means to be an ambassador of Christ today.

For me, I'm hearing two things. First, I will not know that I am Christian because I follow a set of rules, am somehow happier, more successful, or have an easier life. I know I am Christian because I believe in Jesus Christ. My faith is what does it.

But, it doesn't end there. If my calling is to live my life so I am known as an ambassador of Christ, I need to remember to do the things in my life that will ease the suffering of others. There is a difference between knowing and being known. I know I am Christ's ambassador because of my faith. I am known as Christ's ambassador by the impact I have on others.

Let us know. And let us be known.

Amen.

Third Sunday in Lent

1 Corinthians 1:18-25

A Little Foolishness

Hap enjoyed reading his Bible. It wasn't really reading the Bible that he enjoyed, but it was the list of little bits of information he could find that he could use later to trip-up some poor preacher who didn't know those little bits. That's what he enjoyed. And he wasn't really reading his Bible, but excavating, it looking for those little treasures he could use to pose his questions. When he wasn't sitting in his chair reading his King James version, he was out running around town looking for preachers. Hap didn't drive a car but rode a bicycle through the streets, and when necessary, the alleyways that some preachers learned to travel by. The preachers in town all knew about Hap. Most of them had been cornered by him at some point, the lucky ones when they were on their own somewhere without an audience to watch their suffering. The people who lived in houses next door to the church parsonages used to smile and laugh a bit when they saw the preacher suddenly drop the rake in the yard and run to the house. They had apparently seen Hap turn the corner on his bicycle and heading their way. The slow or less-observant ones usually got caught.

Hap would pull up silently behind them and say, "Hey Rev'rund. I've got a question for you. Shadrach, Meshach, and Abednego — who was the oldest?" Then he just stood there waiting, with a smile on his face. Most preachers recognized the names of the three young men thrown into the fiery furnace by King Nebuchadnezzar, but regardless of denomination, none could ever remember what the book of Daniel had said about their ages. Some would just guess, and if they were lucky enough to guess correctly, the waiting question was, "How do you know that?" Most were more upfront and said something like, "No one knows. The story doesn't tell us their ages." The waiting response was something like, "I didn't think you would know. And you call yourself a preacher!" Either way, Hap would then explain that it was obvious that Shadrach was the eldest of the group because when a list of names was written in the Bible the list always put the eldest first. "Just look at all those begats there in Leviticus," Hap would say. "It's all right there in the book!"

The victims might try to redeem themselves by explaining that the lists in Leviticus were written for a specific purpose and weren't there to establish some rule about age, but it was no use. Hap wasn't listening. He would simply shake his head as he quoted from First Corinthians, "I will destroy the wisdom of the wise, the intelligence of the intelligent I will frustrate!"(1 Corinthians 1:19 NIV) and ride off on his search for another preacher.

On Sundays at noon, Hap watched television. That's when the local channel aired the show with the panel of area preachers. Viewers were invited to send in questions, and if you could submit a question the preachers could not answer the station would send you a record album of gospel music. It was Hap's favorite show. When Hap died and his family went in to clean the house, they opened a closet to find a stack of record albums almost four feet high. None of them had been opened. Hap didn't send in his questions so he could listen to music.

For Hap, it wasn't about how much the preachers knew or how well they understood the Bible. It had nothing to do with knowledge or wisdom at all. For Hap, it was all about position. It was about us and them. Hap was from the west end of town where the houses were small, the families were poor, and the graduation diplomas were few and far between. The preachers he sought represented those who saw themselves as something more, who believed they were 'better than' people like Hap. Hap had seen it in their eyes. He had heard it in the way they spoke to him. He had seen it in the looks those people gave his family on Sunday mornings when they sat in their pews with their west end clothing. The preachers represented all those people who looked down on Hap, and those like him.

So Hap made it his mission to knock them down a notch. And since education and wisdom helped those people feel so superior, that's what Hap went after. It was Hap's way of humbling those who had position, who wore the robes in the pulpits and the fancy clothes in the pews; those who looked at Hap and those like him and saw them as different; as something less. It wasn't about wisdom, it was about something else.

Actually, it was exactly what Paul was writing about to the church in Corinth. Hap didn't realize it, but he was interpreting today's passage far better than any of the preachers were, and better than we do most of the time. When we hear Paul say that God will destroy the wisdom of the wise, we usually think he is actually talking about wisdom, that somehow, God thinks it is better to not be wise. I've heard those words used to criticize those who try to understand their faith, who ask questions. I've heard those words be used to tell people they need to quit asking those questions, to stop questioning and thinking about their faith and just believe. Maybe you've heard that too. Maybe you've been told that. But that's not what Paul was saying to the church at Corinth. Paul was doing what Hap was doing.

Corinth was a big city made up of people from all around the world, but at its core it was Greek. That meant much of the city's culture was based on Greek culture, which saw learning and education as something to be sought. We've all heard of the various Greek philosophers like Socrates, Plato, Aristotle, Pythagoras, and the many others who established the long list of schools and academies throughout Corinth. Being a student of one of these schools was a big part of what earned you your position in town; the higher the standing of your teacher, the higher your position or rank in town. And the higher your position, the better you were treated, the more opportunities you were given, the more stuff you got, and the more important you became. In Corinth, people were known by their wisdom.

But wisdom had conditions. Schools and academies charged money. The better the philosopher, the higher the cost. And since the schools and academies had reputations to worry about, there were other requirements to get in, one of which was your family background. If you did not have the cash, or if you came from a family from the west end of town, you did not get in the academy. You did not get an education. You did not get an important teacher. You did not get the position or rank. You did not get better treatment. You did not get the opportunities. You did not get the stuff. You did not become important. In Corinth, you were known as someone less wise than the others. You were known as less important. You were known as less. You were like Hap.

The church in Corinth was different. It did not charge money and it did not have family background requirements. It is no surprise then that many of those who came to the church were those in Corinth who were seen as less important or less wise. To the rest of Corinth, they were seen as the foolish; especially since they believed in something so unwise as the idea that the man Jesus was crucified and then came back to life. That was not the type of thinking that was practiced at the academies. It was foolish thinking, the philosophy of fools.

When Paul wrote to the church in Corinth about wisdom and fools, he wasn't talking about actual intelligence or mental abilities. He was not saying that wisdom was bad, or that it was somehow better to not learn. He was writing to a group of people who were being criticized and attacked because they believed in something that the rest of the city thought was foolish. They were laughed at. They were threatened. They were attacked and beaten. They lost their jobs. They were treated the way someone might be treated if they were seen as being less valuable than someone else.

To some of the wise people of Corinth, the Christians were people who could have made more of themselves if they had really wanted. They could have worked harder to find the money for an education. Maybe they couldn't get into a Socrates academy, but there were plenty of others for that type of person. They were apparently just lazy, and were expecting the rest of the city to take care of them rather than just knuckling down and doing the work like the rest of us — us wise people.

To some of the wise people of Corinth, the poor Christians were living the lives that God wanted them to be living. They were getting what they deserved. That's just how things were, and they just needed to accept the fact that some people were different. They need to make the best of it and not try to become something more than they really were.

As a result, many of the church members were leaving the church, giving up their belief in Jesus Christ, because it hurt too much to be seen as foolish. The hope that came with faith in Jesus Christ was something out of their reach. They just gave it up and accepted the reality that they were, and always would be, less.

That is what Paul was writing to Corinth about. Yes, he said the message of the cross seem pure foolishness to the wise. And they were right about that. It did sound foolish to them. But, the simple reality is that their idea of foolishness was exactly what Jesus expects of us if we are going to live our lives like his.

What is this foolish message of the cross?

It is the foolishness to believe that every person has the same value. I mean, just look around. But, hey — what about that woman on the corner with that cardboard sign? That little kid in the detention camp? What about the woman with the three kids in the basement of that old house trying to live off of a welfare check that she gets from someone else's taxes or that guy with the political ideas that make your stomach turn? That person you see in the congregation each Sunday morning and wonder why they don't clean themselves up a bit more or pick out something a bit nicer to wear? What if we stack them up beside that millionaire? Beside that doctoral degreed person with the books and awards? What about that coiffed and styled family who drives to church each Sunday in the nice car from the best side of town? The ones beside that couple who were raised to know how to work good jobs, pay the taxes, and still save for retirement? Do they really have the same value? Think about it. That's foolish. There is us, and there is them.

It is foolish to think we are all of equal value. It is foolish to think that we all deserve the same thing. We are foolish to think that none of the stuff matters: our roles, houses, clothes, education, looks, that none of it makes any of us any more or less than anyone else. That is foolish.

But... that is the message of the cross. Jesus ended up hanging on the same pole as the criminals and beggars, and he died just like they did. He could have done it differently. He could have rallied his forces, called down a few angels, and kicked the Pharisees, Sadducees, and the Romans all the way down to Antarctica if he had wanted. But the message of the cross would have been that it takes power and powerful actions for God to consider you worth saving. Jesus could have climbed down from the cross, gone back to the temple, and argued theology with the priests and the others, convinced every last one of them that he was right and they were wrong, and then gone to Rome and done the same thing with Caesar. But the message of the cross would have been that it takes human wisdom and the ability to speak and debate for God to consider you worth saving. Maybe Jesus could have even gone straight to Rome and offered Caesar a god-sized boatload of money and bought his freedom. But the message of the cross would have been that you need a lot of stuff for God to consider you worth saving.

Instead, Jesus died alongside those who had nothing, and to the rest of the world, were worth nothing.

It was foolish.

It still is foolish.

Think about it the next time you pull up to the traffic light and see that woman with cardboard sign, the millionaire, the photo of the child in the detention camp, the doctorate, the lady and her kids in that basement, the guy with the political beliefs, the family driving in from the good side of town, the person not dressed the way you think they might be, or the couple with the nice house and retirement plan. What goes through your mind when you see them? What do you see?

As an ambassador of Christ, a person living your life the way you believe Jesus would live it, what do you see?

Amen.

[Note to the preacher: Hap in this story was real, as was his bicycle and the fear he put into the community's preachers. Hap was my grandfather. The stack of record albums was real too.]

Liz

The church had received a nice donation from a member who wanted to help the church expand its youth ministry. The board decided that the best use of the money would be to hire a full-time youth leader; someone who could relate to the youth and help create an active program. A committee was formed to find that person and bring their recommendation back to next month's board meeting. At that meeting, the committee was happy to announce they have found what they thought was the perfect person to lead the new ministry, and they were even more excited to say it was someone from their own community. They recommended Liz.

There were nods of approval and smiles. Until they all heard the big sigh, followed by "You *have* to be kidding — Liz?" And then it began.

Liz was in her early twenties. She had been attending the church regularly for the past year or so. Both Liz and her three-year-old daughter attended Sunday school. Liz volunteered to bake pies for the annual bazaar. Liz was popular with the youth of the church. The committee listed these points before some of the others around the table joined in.

They reminded everyone that Liz's parents had had nothing but trouble with her. She ran around and got in trouble in school. She hung out with the wrong crowd in town and ended up having to get married. That guy she married was no good and he ended up in jail, leaving Liz to take care of her daughter. She found a part-time job down at the café, but couldn't find anything more than that. It was wonderful that she and her daughter were taking part in the church; they certainly needed it.

But lead the church's youth program? Did the board really believe that Liz was the type of person we wanted to hold up as an example for the youth in our church? What kind of message would we be giving them? Sure, go ahead, do whatever you want. Run around, do your own thing, and when you get in enough trouble just come crawling back and we'll pretend like none of it ever happened. Is that what this church wants to say to our young people?

It went back and forth from there. Part of the board supported Liz for the role and others thought it was absolutely the wrong idea. The pastor said a few words about forgiveness and how the church is the one place where we are given a new chance. The pastor said the church could do a tremendous thing for Liz by giving her this opportunity to minister to the kids. The pastor was told to be realistic. The naysayers said they were not going to let our kids be led astray by someone like Liz. She was welcome to come to church and seek forgiveness, but to lead the church's youth? Absolutely not.

The board meeting ended that night without a youth minister. Most board members did not know that the anonymous donor behind the new role was one of the people sitting quietly at the table. After the meeting, she spoke with the pastor. She shook her head and said she had no idea some in the church felt as they did. And, if that was the attitude of the church, she would do something more meaningful with the gift herself. She would just give it to Liz directly.

This is the same situation that the writer of our scripture passage today was addressing at the church in Ephesus. No, it wasn't about hiring a youth leader, but it was about deciding what it means to be a part of the church. Was there a criterion that defined what it meant to be worthy of salvation, and if so, what was it? Those in the church who converted from Judaism insisted that to be a true Christian you first had to obey the old laws of Moses. Men had to be circumcised. You could not eat certain foods. You could not sit at a table with anyone who did eat food that was impure. You might attend church every week and bring pies to the annual bazaar, but if you did not follow the old laws you were not truly Christian.

The gentile members had come from all kinds of backgrounds, filled with things that may not have been all that good. But even those who had been Jewish knew full well there were plenty of law-abiding Jews who were just as corrupt as any gentile; remember the Pharisees, the Sadducees, and the priests?

What do we need to do to be saved? What are the rules we must follow? What if we have a questionable past? What do we do to earn back the right to be a full-blown Christian? What can someone like Liz do to be accepted as one of us? Us being the true members of First Church Ephesus.

This is why most of the letter to the Ephesians sounded like Christianity 101. The letter said, several times, that every person in the Ephesian church had been dead and lost. Every last one of them, no matter what they ate, who they ate with, or what other laws or rituals they might have obeyed or not obeyed. None of them had a background that could earn them a pew in the church. Not a one.

And insisting that everyone follow those rules and laws now, or insisting that those with a questionable background stand over in the corner for a while, wasn't going to make any difference either. Being a Christian isn't something you deserve or not. The salvation that Jesus offers isn't something you earn. It is something that is given. No matter what anyone thinks we might deserve, it is given simply because we are loved.

Today's passage says something you have probably heard before: we are saved by grace, not by works. We cannot do enough, own enough, learn enough, or give enough to deserve to be accepted. We cannot keep score of our work to see that we are more deserving than anyone else. Those board members sitting around the table wearing their Sunday school fifty-year perfect attendance pins on their collars had earned no more salvation than Liz did. The writer said that God raised up the people of Ephesus like he did Jesus. It was God's action, not theirs, that gave them their role as an ambassador for Jesus Christ in Ephesus. It was their faith, not their works.

But we need to be careful with that passage. I have heard people ask, if salvation is a gift and not from us doing anything, then why do we spend so much time worrying about what it means to be a Christian? Why work at it? If we work hard to do good and it's not going to make any difference in our being Christian, why stress over it? If I believe, I am saved. So why not just believe and relax. That's my motto. Chill.

That is probably why the writer of Ephesians added the note,

For we are God's handiwork, created in Christ Jesus to do good works, which God prepared in advance for us to do.

Each person in the church at Ephesus was not only given their salvation without earning it, but each one of them was handcrafted by God to be there as part of the church. Former Jew, gentile, law-follower or law-ignorer, God created them to bring their life experience into the church to do good things. Think about those people sitting around that board meeting table. I can guarantee you that Liz was going to understand things about the youth of that church that no one else around that table was going to understand. She was going to be able to speak with them like none of the rest of them. She was going to be able to minister to them in a very meaningful way because that is what she was created to do. She is what God created her to be so she can pass forward what she alone can.

Followers of Christ don't work to do good things for others to make ourselves better Christians. We do good things for others because we were created to be an ambassador for Christ, and that is what that job calls for. That is the role we have been prepared for. You may not have been prepared the same way I was prepared, but your background gives you the ability to understand and do things I can't understand or do, and mine does the same for me. And whatever path brought us to this place, we both stand as equals here, with an unearned salvation and the job of doing what we can to ease the suffering of and give hope to others.

Let's take some time this week and reflect. If you ever find yourself looking at someone and feeling that they are somehow less worthy, or of less value, remind yourself to spend less time thinking about how you might be able to help them become more worthy, and spend that time remembering that God created them to be an ambassador for Christ, just like you.

Anything else is just a distraction.

Amen.

Who The Heck Is Melchizedek?

There were five kings; joined together to fight for their independence. There was King Bera of Sodom, King Birsha of Gomorrah, King Shinab of Admah, King Shemeber of Zeboiim, and the King of Bela. For the past twelve years, those kings had served the King of Elam, Chedorlaomer. They each ruled their own countries, but they each paid Chedorlaomer for the privilege to do it. Not any longer — the five kings brought their armies together in the Valley of Siddim near the Dead Sea and prepared to fight for their independence.

Chedolaomer did not come to the fight alone. King Arioch of Ellasar and King Tidal of Goiim sent their armies to fight alongside the army of Chedorlaomer. Together, they formed an army that was out to teach a lesson to anyone who might ever think of rebelling against those in power. We read in Genesis fourteen that they didn't wait until they got to the valley to make their point. While the armies of Chedorlaomer and his partners were still on the way to the real fight, they subdued the Rephaim in Ashteroth-karnaim, the Zuzim in Ham, the Emim in Shaveh-kiriathaim, and the Horites in the hill country of Seir as far as El-paran on the edge of the wilderness. On their way back home after the battle, they subdued the Amalekites and Amorites in Hazazon-tamar.

Then they arrived at the Valley of Siddim. Genesis reminds us that the valley of the Dead Sea was a very difficult place. It was not only extremely dry and hot, but the ground was so low it was scattered with places where hot oil seeped up from the earth and created pits of thick tar. Someone not being very careful could find themselves trapped in one of those pits. Even though the rebels brought five armies to fight Chedorlaomer's four, once the fighting began it didn't take long for the rebels to see they were out-classed and their battle for independence was lost. Many were killed. Many tried to flee and fell into a waiting pit of tar. The rest were taken as prisoners.

They didn't just take the army. To make their point even more clear, the armies of Chedorlaomer marched into the cities of the five rebellious countries and took everyone and everything as spoils of war. As they loaded up their prisoners from the city of Sodom, one of the men taken as prisoner was a resident by the name of Lot, the son of a man named Haran. Haran had a brother whose name was Abraham.

Abraham lived near what we now call Hebron, about seventeen miles south of the city known as Salem, that we now call Jerusalem. We're told that someone who had escaped from Chedorlaomer forces found Abraham and told him that his nephew had been taken prisoner. Abraham gathered his trained men, 318 of them, and set off to find the army of Chedorlaomer and set his nephew free. Abraham knew that Chedorlaomer would be heading home to Elam, which was to the west in what is now Iran. He also knew that, instead of traveling west across miles of desert wilderness, the army would first go north along the Great Sea and then turn east to go around the desert. So Abraham and his 318 men began walking north.

One hundred and twenty miles later, near the city called Dan, Abraham's trained men found the five joined armies of King Chedorlaomer. Rather than make the mistake the others had made, Abraham divided his men into groups that traveled through the night and surprised Chedolaomer's army near Damascus. Chadolaomer's army panicked and Abraham's 318 men chased them to a place called Hobah. When the fighting was over, Genesis says that Abraham brought back all of the goods, and the people, and his nephew Lot.

As Abraham and his men walked south to go back home, there were celebrations as they traveled. The countries and families of those people Chedolamer had taken prisoner came out to meet Abraham to thank him for bringing their people home again. As Abraham passed the King's Valley near the city of Salem, the King of Sodom came out to meet him.

Then Melchizedek arrived.

We don't know much about Melchizedek, other than that he was supposedly the King of Salem. We don't know who or where he came from, or what happened to him and where he went. We do know he was actually the High Priest of Salem, but the writers of Genesis called him a king because he was known as the founder of what would become the royal priesthood. And we know that as Abraham and the King of Sodom were meeting in the King's Valley, Melchizedek came out of Salem bringing bread and wine, and a blessing for Abraham. We are told that, in return, Abraham gave him a gift of one-tenth of all of the goods that had been recaptured, and then they all went home.

From that point on, Melchizedek was only mentioned in one verse of Psalm 110, until we find him again in today's passage from Hebrews, where he is mentioned nine times altogether. It just makes you wonder why, after all this time, the writer of Hebrews talked about him — and so much?

Just who the heck is Melchizedek and what does he have to do with us here today?

It might help to understand who the book of Hebrews was written by and who it was written to. First, it's not like many of the other books we have that were written as letters to one specific church in one specific location. Hebrews was more of a sermon than a letter. It was written to those Gentiles and Jews who had joined the early church but were now facing some really difficult times. It was most likely written between the years 60 and 90 when organized persecutions of the church were underway. Beginning around 60 AD, in addition to the attacks from groups with other religions and philosophies, members of the church began to be persecuted by the Roman government. Up to that point, Rome had considered the Christians to be just another sect of Judaism and more of a local thing in a small corner of the Roman Empire. Things changed when Nero became the Roman emperor in the year 54 AD. Hearing the growing Christian community calling Jesus their king was something Nero saw as treason, and that had to be addressed. Whatever actually caused the great fire of Rome in the year 64 AD, Nero blamed it on the Christians as part of their goal to overthrow Rome for their own king. Being a Christian became a deadly thing to do.

Those arrested in Rome and accused of being Christian were given the opportunity to recant their faith and state loudly and clearly that Nero was their one and only king. Those who did not recant were made examples of. Rome knew how to make examples. Just over one hundred years before, a group of slaves had attempted to oppose Rome. As a result, the Appian Way, the road that reached three hundred miles between Rome and Brindisi, was lined on both sides with six thousand crosses, each holding a crucified slave. Rome was very good at making their point. Some people who refused to give up their Christian faith were tied, dipped in tubs of oil, and tied to poles in the main courtyard of Nero's house. That night, those Christians were used as torches to provide the light for Nero's parties. For more and more members of the church, It was just too dangerous to stay.

Staying in the church was made even more difficult as more people argued that even if they did remain true and sacrifice their lives for their faith, it wouldn't do any good because Jesus was not the one who could really help them. He was great, yes, but there were others who were just as great or greater. For those with a Jewish background, there were many people of history who were remembered as the most truthful followers of God, and choosing the right one to follow would to win God's favor. There was Moses. There was Abraham. There was David. And there were others, many of whom were high priests from the temple. For those who came to the church as gentiles, they were familiar with all of the different temples in town, each with their own high priest, some of whom were believed to have great understanding and power.

As a result, many of the members of the early church, even though they believed in Jesus, were still heard to proclaim, "I follow Moses!", "I follow David!", or they followed this high priest or that high priest. While Jesus was great, was he really great enough to die for?

We nod our heads and say, "Of course he is. That's what Easter is all about!" But might there be at least some spark of doubt …? Picture it this way. You wake up in the morning to the sound of the door being broken down. You are bound and taken to a room filled with people dressed in uniforms and carrying weapons. Someone sitting in a big chair calls your name and says he is going to ask you a question and give you one chance to answer it. If you answer it correctly they will take you back home. If you answer it incorrectly, you are going to die. One chance. The question is, "Who do you believe Jesus is? A man, or a king?" What do you say?

I'm not asking that to try and be dramatic or to just make you uncomfortable. Sadly, that is exactly what is happening in too many places today where Christians understand how tempting it can be to put our hope elsewhere and walk away. Those are the people the writer of Hebrews was writing to. He was writing to people who were wondering if Jesus was really the one, or if one of those others might be the better choice. That's why the writer wrote about the old high priest called Melchizedek.

Although very little is written in the Bible about Melchizedek, out of all of the people from history who were remembered as powerful people of the faith, Melchizedek stood at the top. Normally, when two important people met, the lesser important person gave a gift to the more important one. Who gave the gift when Abraham met Melchizedek? Abraham did. So who was even greater than Father Abraham? Melchizedek. Since many considered Abraham to be even more important than all the others like Moses and David, that meant Melchizedek was greater than all of them.

Some believed that since nothing was known about where Melchizedek came from or where he went after meeting Abraham, he was not just another high priest, but he was a heavenly being. sent from God to give Abraham that blessing he gave. Not only was he greater than all of the historic men of the faith, but he was greater than any other high priest from any other temple on earth. So, if you are looking for someone to put your faith in, Melchizedek is at the very top of that list.

The writer of Hebrews said,

We have this hope, a sure and steadfast anchor of the soul, a hope that enters the inner shrine behind the curtain, where Jesus, a forerunner on our behalf, has entered, having become a high priest forever according to the order of Melchizedek.

(Hebrews 6:19-20)

Just to make his point, the writer reminded his readers about that curtain in the temple that separates the holiest room of the temple from the rest. No one passed that curtain into the holy of holies except the high priest, and he did that only once a year, very quickly, to replace candles and incense. But Jesus passed that curtain and entered that room, where no one else ever entered. Even the gentile members understood that because even their temples had their own protected, sacred rooms.

We are fortunate to come here today without the fear of being dragged into a room and being forced to make a life or death choice about Jesus. But we do have those moments when following him as his ambassador is a painful thing to do. Those moments when we feel that spark of a question: is he really the one?

Who the heck is Melchizedek? He's the one who gives us the answer to our question.

Amen.

Hosanna!

Let's remember the story the way we've been told it.

Even though the sun was just beginning to peek over the mountains to the east, if you looked at the highway climbing up from the Jordan Valley, you could see the lines of people coming to Jerusalem for Passover. One of the highlights of the Jewish faith was making the annual journey to Jerusalem for Passover and make your sacrifice at the temple. They came from all corners of the world, filling the streets with noise and excitement. On one of those narrow streets of the village of Bethany near the top of the mountain, Jesus stood outside the door and watched as people passing by stopped and began to gather around him and his disciples. This is what happened after his reputation had grown. The crowd gathered to hear what instruction he would offer that morning, or if he might even perform another miracle. As the crowd began to fill the street, it grew quiet; waiting.

Then Jesus stepped from the doorway and began walking. He walked up the street, up the dusty road toward the top of the hill. The crowd followed, tugging the robes of the disciples to ask what he was going to do. Where was he going? Was he going to teach? At one point, Jesus turned and said something to one of the disciples who quickly slipped away.

When Jesus reached Bethphage near the top of the mountain, he stopped. From where they stood, they could see the city of Jerusalem. They could see the Jerusalem temple just across the Kidron Valley with its golden columns shining in the sunlight just breaking over the hill where Jesus stood on top.

From across the Kidron Valley, the Roman Centurions stood guard on the walls of the temple and could see the crowd on the hill.

Jesus stood quietly at the top of the hill and looked at the temple. The crowd grew larger as people from the valley side of the mountain saw Jesus coming and ran to join him. They spoke a lot of different languages, but they were all asking the same thing, "What is he doing to do?"

The disciple came back, leading a donkey along with its small colt.

The noise began somewhere in the middle of the crowd. Someone immediately made the connection with the passage from the book of Zechariah,

Rejoice greatly, Daughter Zion!
Shout, Daughter Jerusalem!
See, your king comes to you,
righteous and victorious,
lowly and riding on a donkey,
on a colt, the foal of a donkey.

(Zechariah 9:9)

More people caught on as someone spread robes across the back of the donkey and Jesus climbed on. "King!" someone said. "He is going into Jerusalem as the king!" Some in the crowd picked up branches from the palm trees and began waving them in the air. Zechariah wrote about the king of peace and the palm branch was a symbol of peace. Some started shouting "Hosanna" because Zecharaiah's king of peace was coming to save or rescue them.

The centurions watched as the crowd moved down the hill toward the city. They could see the waving branches and hear the shouting. The centurions didn't care about what Zechariah had written about a king of peace. They didn't care about any of that religious stuff. All they cared about was keeping things under control so nothing violent happened that Caesar might hear about back in Rome and get all upset. As long as the group behaved themselves, let them come.

The centurions watched as the crowd crossed the Kidron, moved up the hill to the temple and Jesus got off the donkey and walked through the eastern gate. The crowd followed but got a bit quieter as they walked between the rows of armored and armed centurians.

Exactly what happened next isn't all that clear. At some point, Jesus walked over to the group of moneylenders where people from out of town could exchange their form of currency into the money that was used at the temple. Everyone knew the moneylenders charged unfair rates for exchange, but they couldn't do anything about it because the lenders were in cahoots with the temple leaders, who got a cut of the take. We're told that's when Jesus crossed the line as far as the centurions were concerned. He stopped walking and talking and started turning things over and throwing them. He apparently either stopped before the centurions felt they had to intervene, or the centurions held back because the crowd with Jesus was too big. But either way, Jesus had crossed that line for the centurions and they now agreed with the temple leaders that something had to be done about this Jesus guy.

But the crowd was alive. They cheered as Jesus argued with the temple leaders, the Pharisees, and the Sadducees. They cheered as Jesus looked at the magnificent temple and said that very soon there would not be one stone left standing. They cheered as they walked past the centurion guards, back across the Kidron Valley, up the hill and back to Bethany. They cheered as most of them forgot about Zechariah's king being the king of peace, and celebrated the fact that King Jesus had just walked right into the center of the enemy and had taken the first steps to grind them into the dust. This Jesus was a king of power. This Jesus was a king of justice, of righteousness. Jesus was here to show what God did with those who disobeyed. The crowds and the disciples couldn't wait to see what he was going to do next.

We frequently call this the story of the triumphal entry — a day of victory — the day Jesus rode boldly into Jerusalem, called out the crooked moneylenders and temple leaders, stared Rome in the face and proclaimed his true power. Sometimes we look at Palm Sunday as an example of what the church is called to do when it is confronted with things it disagrees with. We sometimes see Palm Sunday as a reminder that, sometimes, we as Christians and as the church need to stand up, wave our branches, shout our words, walk right into the middle of those we disagree with and start throwing things around. It seems that, sometimes, it takes some yelling and throwing to create peace.

Then we read the lines from the letter to the Philippians,

In your relationships with one another, have the same mindset as Christ Jesus.
Taking the very nature of a servant.
He made himself nothing.
He humbled himself by becoming obedient to death.

(Philippians 2:5-8)

It makes me wonder if we, as people called to be ambassadors for Jesus Christ, might need to take another look at the story of Palm Sunday. Is the story any different if we think about it with Jesus' mindset? If we saw it through his eyes? It doesn't really change the story; what happened, happened. It might give us a little different understanding of what was really going on, and what it might mean for us now.

Let us remember what Matthew said happened as they were all on their way to Jerusalem those few days before. Jesus had been teaching about the kingdom of God. He told them that when they got to Jerusalem he was going to be delivered to the priests, he would be condemned to death, he would be crucified, but three days later he would be resurrected. That is what was going to happen; what had to happen for him to fulfill his role. It is why he was here. Whatever happened on that Palm Sunday, Jesus' mindset was that he had to be arrested and crucified. Nothing else mattered.

Moneylenders didn't matter. Crooked priests didn't matter. Centurions and even Rome didn't matter. As wrong as those things were, it was not his role to deal with them. He had to die.

I have to wonder. As he rode that donkey down the hill in the middle of that crowd, was he thinking about a king in a procession, or was he thinking something like, "Yeah, this ought to get them worried enough to do something about me." When he turned over those moneylender tables, was he just thinking what Matthew said about a den of robbers, or was he also thinking, "Now the centurions are going to have to do something to stop me"? When he told the crowd that the temple would soon be destroyed, was he just thinking about a miraculous destruction, or was he also thinking, "There is no way they are doing to let me live now that I've threatened the temple itself?"

Honestly, I don't know what if Jesus actually thought any of these things, but it seems they fit the way of thinking that the scripture presents. Jesus did not come to just overthrow a few crooked leaders or clean up a few unethical business people. Jesus was sent to die for our sins. Whatever else was going on, his role was to do what he was sent to do.

If that might be true, is it possibly true for us as well? Whatever else might be going on, our role is to do what we were called to do; to be an ambassador for Christ. It is to live our lives as he lived his. Is it possible that, rather than march, yell, and threaten each other about a few specific issues, we are to take the very nature of a servant, to make ourselves nothing, to being obedient, even to death?

Is it possible that we do not have to be right? Is it possible that we do not have to win the argument or have to even protect the church? All we have to do is do what we have been called to do. We have to love.

Hosanna!

Amen.

1 Corinthians 11:23-26

Passover Or Passalong?

They had done this before. Some of their earliest memories were of their families celebrating the Passover Seder. It was a high point of the year. It was also a celebration that involved every member of the family, from youngest to eldest, they all played a role. The adults would read the important lines of the ritual, the younger would take turns asking the required questions, and the youngest would join in the search for the hidden matzo that represented desert. As they joined around the table tonight, their thoughts were a mix of what had been happening this week, over the past three years together, and all of those memories of seders gone by.

They knew the parts of the seder and what they represented. They remembered the laughter from the adults that first time they had gulped down that mouthful of horseradish that represented the suffering and tears their ancestors had experienced. They remembered how it felt like ages before the ritual allowed them to take another drink to wash the burning away. They remembered the vegetables, the shank bone, and the stew that came from it. They remembered the bread that had been made so quickly it was more like a dry cracker than the bread they usually ate. They remembered the cup that sat in front of the person leading the seder. The cup that was put there for Elijah.

They knew the story behind it all. They remembered how their ancestors had been slaves in Egypt until God sent Moses to set them free. They could recite the list of plagues that Moses performed, ending with the tenth, the one that was the reason they were at the table. That plague that finally caused the Pharoah to let God's people go free. The plague that sent God himself down that night to travel through the streets of Egypt killing every firstborn son in Egypt except in those houses who followed the instructions. Those families gathered around their tables and ate the meal to celebrate the fact that God had passed over their house and spared them from the final plague. That is how they survived, escaped, and became the people they were today. Tonight, as they ate the food and drank the wine, they remembered it all.

For the disciples, meeting around the tables for the seder that night was a welcomed break from the stress. The past few years had been difficult as they followed Jesus around, but they now looked like a vacation compared to what had been happening since they came to Jerusalem four days ago. No matter where they went now, people were shouting to them; some cheering them on and some demanding they be arrested. This room they sat in tonight felt so quiet, so safe, it allowed them to relax. The seder was familiar. The seder was something that gave them a sense of comfort, a sense of being a part of God's people

Until Jesus came to the part of the seder called the Yachatz, the breaking of the bread. The person leading the ritual had a plate in front of them, holding three flat pieces of matzah. The middle matzah would be picked up and torn in half. It was called the "bread of poverty" and in a few minutes would be shared and eaten as they retold the story of the Exodus. This broken matzah reminded them of how broken they had been, and how God had divided the sea to help them get to freedom and make them whole once again.

The disciples seemed a bit confused when Jesus changed the words. As he passed the broken matzah around the table, he told them from now on whenever they eat it they should think about him and how it now represented what was going to happen to his body very soon. Suddenly, the quiet room no longer felt as safe as it had before.

Things may have settled down again for a while, until the end of the seder when Jesus picked up the fifth cup. The room went quiet. The seder included drinking four glasses of wine as part of the ritual, but there was a fifth glass on the table; the Elijah cup. It was filled and placed in front of the seder leader, but it was left untouched. The tradition was clear that one of these nights during a seder, the prophet Elijah would appear to announce that the Messiah was about to appear. Near the end of the seder, the door to the room would be opened briefly and everyone would hold their breath and watch to see if this was the year Elijah would enter and drink his cup of wine. The Elijah cup would remain untouched until that night came.

Jesus picked up the fifth cup. He not only picked it up, but he drank from it. He not only drank from it, but he passed it around the table and told them all to drink. As they drank from the cup, instead of thinking about Elijah, they were asked to think about Jesus' own blood that was about to be shed. Can you imagine seeing their faces as the cup was passed to them? Can you imagine their faces as they held that cup that had been untouchable for so many years? Can you imagine what they were feeling?

It wasn't about just remembering the broken past and setting out a cup in the hope that, one of these days, somebody might show up at that open door and tell us there was hope. We come to this table remembering that hope has become reality; we break the bread to remember that Jesus could have kept his body from being broken but he did not; we drink from the cup to remember that Jesus could have kept his blood from dripping down that cross but he did not. We gather here now to celebrate that we have been invited to God's table. We didn't earn the invitation. We are here because of Jesus' body and blood, that's all. We are here because we were given a seat at this table. We are welcome here, equal here, and we have hope here. When we let ourselves think about it, it still feels kind of magical, and perhaps for just a few, brief minutes, we feel what the disciples felt that night it happened for the first time; what it feels like to be the people of God.

I read today's passage from Corinthians.

Paul started this church some time ago, and it has now been around long enough for people to start getting a bit distracted. That's what happens sometimes, isn't it? We start off all excited about our faith and working together to do good things, then things change. We may share the same faith, but there are a lot of other things we look at very differently, and as time passes, those things get all tangled up in our faith, and we start focusing more on our differences than on that faith that brought us together in the first place. Paul was writing to remind them of that faith; that faith that made them the church in the first place and was more important than any of the distractions.

He wrote to remind them what it really means to come together at the Lord's table as one people — one church. He described the way they were behaving and reminded them of the way they ought to be behaving. But that's not the part that is bothering me. The part I can't get out of my head is the first line. When I first read it I just kind of passed over it as his introduction to the really important stuff. Maybe it was the same for you? Remember what he said?

> *For I received from the Lord what I also passed on to you….*
> (1 Corinthians 11:23 NIV)

It sounds pretty basic, doesn't it? Paul was just telling them that what he was about to tell them was not something he made up but what actually happened. He was telling them what others told him. That's not what *my* mind is hearing. I hear those words asking me a question. What I hear is, "You have received a place at this table. No matter who you used to be, or what you may have done before, you have received acceptance as a child of God. You did not earn it. God has given you a new life." Then Paul looks me right in the eyes and asks, "Is that what you have passed along to everyone else or have some been passed over?"

Now, I have to be honest and say that I don't have any evidence at all that Paul was actually intending to ask us that when he first wrote the words. I think his mind was on the divided church in Corinth. But still, as I prepare to take my unearned place at the table now, I hear the words asking if I have held anything back in my role as Christ's ambassador. Are there people I have met that I held back some of my compassion? Did I see them and make assumptions that caused me to not care as deeply as I could have for them, and I passed over the opportunity to give them the love I could have given them? Are there people I don't even know because I have, for some reason, thought they were so different from me, thought they were not worth knowing? Are there people with lives so misdirected that I thought they were too far beyond inviting them to share an unearned seat at this table? Have I passed along to others what I received from God, or have I just passed along a few pieces here, and a few pieces there, as I believed those pieces were deserved?

I was really looking forward to coming to the table here and relaxing and feeling peace of mind as I joined with others in God's family. But what I am honestly thinking about is the body and blood that gave me a seat at this table, and if there are others somewhere outside the door who should be here with me, but I did not open that door wide enough to let them.

For I received from the Lord what I also passed on to you...

Or have I?
Amen.

Good Friday

Hebrews 10:16-25

Click To Unfriend

Mary Magdalene stood at the edge of the road and cried. She knew this was going to happen. Jesus had told them over and over that he would be arrested and killed. She thought she had prepared herself for it but she was not at all prepared for what had actually happened. As she stood at the edge of the road, her eyes moving back and forth from the men lowering his body from that cross to his mother standing just behind them watching it happen. She thought about all that had happened since last night.

After the disciples had celebrated the seder, they all walked out of Jerusalem and met in the olive garden just across the Kidron Brook, in a place called Gethsemane. Jesus and the disciples went off by themselves into the garden while the rest of the group found places to try and get some rest. It wasn't as comfortable as going back to the house in Bethany again, but the week had been difficult and they needed to be out and away from the crowds and what they were stirring up. It was a few hours later when most were asleep that Mary had been awakened by the noise from the garden. She was outside the garden wall, but some say a few men had appeared, while others said it was a large group of soldiers, but the crowds with them were so large it was hard to tell who was really in control of it. All she knew was that they had come for Jesus, and they took him away.

Then she saw Judas following the group up the road toward the city. Earlier, she had seen him leave the seder room before it was over, but didn't know why until someone told her when they got to the garden. She followed them toward the city as well, watching for the other disciples to try and find out what had actually happened and where they were going. She followed the crowd to the courtyard outside the meeting place of the Sanhedrin, the Jewish Supreme Court. That's when she saw Peter. She crept up to speak with him when she saw a servant girl approach him. The girl said that she recognized him as one of the men with Jesus. Peter waved her away and said he didn't know what she was talking about. Mary stopped. Another servant girl said that she recognized him too, and Peter turned away and said he didn't even know the man. Mary stared. A few people were standing nearby and hear them said they recognized his Galilean accent and they were sure that he was one of those following Jesus. Peter raised his voice and swore at them, saying that he didn't even know the man.

Mary turned away.

The crowd started moving again. It was a bit easier to see now that the sun was coming up, but there were just too many people for her to get close enough to see Jesus himself and find out what was happening to him. She stayed near the back of the crowd until they came to the gates of the house of the governor, Pontius Pilate. She heard the accusations and arguments and her breath was taken away when she heard them all given the opportunity to have Jesus set free but they wanted the criminal Barabbas freed instead. She looked for the other disciples but did not see them. If they were here, they were staying quiet, and safe. She heard the crowds getting louder, shouting "Crucify him!" The word exploded in her mind. Even though she remembered Jesus telling them this would happen, she heard herself scream "NO!" But no one heard her or even cared. Mary watched as Barabbas was brought out and turned loose, while Jesus was taken away by a group of Roman Centurians. She fought through the crowd to keep up with them until they reached the Antonia Fortress where she watched as he was taken inside and the gates shut behind them.

As the morning passed and became afternoon she tried to find people who could tell her what was happening inside the fortress; what was happening to Jesus. All she heard were bits and pieces, but it was enough to terrify her. She approached one soldier leaving the fortress who said the soldiers had taken Jesus to play the king's game. Mary had heard rumors of the game. There was a series of little squares carved on the stone floor of the fortress and the soldiers would throw dice to move their game piece along the squares until someone reached the final square. The winner of each round got to choose from a list of punishments to give to the prisoner. After all of the other actions on the list had been won, the prisoner was ready for crucifixion.

The game would last much of the day. As soldiers came and went, Mary learned that Jesus had been flogged. They had taken off his robe, tied his arms around a large pole, and whipped him with a stick that had long pieces of leather straps on it, each strap with a small piece of bone or metal on it. The pieces of leather tore flesh where they struck. The solder smiled as he described what had happened. Mary wept.

She learned that the next winner always selected the robe. They would take a dirty blanket from the stable and drape it over the back and shoulders of the prisoner, pressing it into the flogging wounds. Then, they would rip it off again, put it back on, rip it back off, over and over until they grew tired of it.

She later heard that one of the soldiers playing the game had selected the crown. They made a round crown out of branches from a bush often called firethorn; a large, mildly poisonous bush covered with sharp thorns. The crown would be made slightly smaller than the prisoner's head and forced to fit down over the forehead.

It was late afternoon when the doors to the Antonia Fortress opened and Mary saw the soldiers come out. She saw Jesus. He was moving slowly, bent under the weight of the large piece of wood he was dragging. She could see the blood running down his face from the crown and more dried on the back of the blanket covering his back. She followed them through the crowded streets and listened to the people laughing and mocking him. Some yelled that he didn't look much like the king of the Jews now. She searched the crowd for the disciples but didn't see them. Near the city gate, Jesus stumbled, and she saw the soldiers pull a man from the crowd to help him support the weight of the large board. She found out later he was from Cyrene in Africa, and his name was Simon.

She followed the group through the city gate to the side of the old stone quarry that had been turned into a cemetery. There was a large column of rock in the middle of the quarry, made of stone that was not good enough to be worth digging out. The column had a strange shape, almost like a skull, and it was close enough to the road for everyone passing by could see it, so it was the ideal place for crucifixions. That is where the soldiers were heading. When they reached the top, they placed the heavy board across the large pole lying on the ground and tied them together. Then they forced Jesus to lay down and stretch his arms on the board. They drove nails through his arms into the board.

Three soldiers began lifting the long pole while others guided the other end into the hole in the rock. They lifted until the weight of the pole took over and it began sliding until it slammed against the bottom of the hole. The soldiers laughed as Jesus' body jerked from the force and began to sag under its own weight, pulling against the nails. A soldier held Jesus' feet up sideways against the pole while another drove the nails through them into the pole. This would keep some of the weight off of his hands and not tear them, which might end the suffering far too quickly. One soldier held the dirty blanket he had remembered to tear from Jesus' back to make sure the rough pole pressed against the still open wounds.

Mary stayed and watched it all.

She heard the words Jesus spoke. She saw someone hold the damp sponge to his dried lips, promising the relief of cool water but delivering instead bitter vinegar.

She was there when he died.

She watched as the soldiers dropped his body from the cross and Joseph of Arimathea and others picked it up before the soldiers could throw it from the column into the trash pile below as they usually did. She watched as they placed the body in one of the tombs dug into the side of the quarry, one that belonged to Joseph's family. She watched them wrap Jesus' body in a clean cloth. It was getting late, and the soldiers were under orders to guard the tomb, so Joseph and the others decided to come back and finish the burial preparations later. Tomorrow was the sabbath, so they would have to wait until Sunday morning to come back and do that. Mary watched as Joseph rolled the stone door closed, and two centurions took their places in front of it.

Mary Magdalene stood at the edge of the road and cried. She thought she had prepared herself for it but she was not at all prepared for what had actually happened. She moved her eyes back and forth from the column in the middle of the quarry to his mother who stood near the guards. She was not at all prepared.

Mary turned and walked through the city gate. She walked quietly through the crowded streets until she came to the coffee shop. She ordered a latte, sat down, and pulled out her phone. She opened Facebook® and searched for Peter's name. When she found it, she clicked "Unfriend." She did the same with Judas, and with each of the other disciples. Then she opened Twitter® and did the same thing. After what they had done, it was what they deserved.

Of course, I just made up that last little part there. We don't know what Mary actually did after the crucifixion, but it wasn't going for a latte and using social media. All of the rest of the story is true, and I certainly don't mean to make light of it with that little fiction at the end.

But I am trying to help us understand something Paul said in that passage we have from his letter to the Hebrews. The church was disillusioned, like Mary. They had believed they were all prepared for what it meant to be the church but they had discovered they were not. The church began as a collection of new Christians, a mixture of former gentiles and former Jews, but they all understood that the most important thing for them to do was be leave the past behind and live new lives as Jesus intended them to live.

But they weren't prepared.

They were arguing with each other. They argued over old traditions and rules, they argued about new traditions and rules, and they argued about what it meant to live as Jesus would live. They split into groups, with this group not talking with that group and this group not going to the same church service as the other. If they would have had Facebook® and Twitter®, they would most certainly have unfriended each other. The greatest threat to the people Paul wrote to in Hebrews was not the pressure from outside the church, but from division inside the church. That is what he wrote about.

He said they should not give up meeting together as some of them were apparently doing. He said that instead of arguing they should be encouraging each other now more than ever. If they were going to provoke each other, they should provoke each other to love and do good things. Rather than divide ourselves and only associate with those people who agree with us on everything, we should focus on the simple fact that the crucifixion of Jesus put an end to any form of division.

Paul reminded them of the curtain.

The temple in Jerusalem was made up of different sections. The open area outside was open to anyone who wanted to come. But there was a fence inside that anyone who was not Jewish could not cross. Inside the fence, there was a wall separating the spaces that no one could enter unless they were a priest. And there was the curtain — the huge curtain hung over the entrance to the central room of the temple, the holy of holies. It was a small sanctuary that could only be entered once a year, and only by the high priest on the Day of Atonement when he sprinkled blood on the altar. The carefully embroidered curtain was almost four inches thick and separated the holy from the holier. It represented the division that existed between holy and unholy, between God and people.

Paul reminded the Hebrews that the moment Jesus died, that holy curtain, the veil dividing God from people, was torn in two from top to bottom. The death of Jesus on the cross ended division between God and people, and between people and people. It is the message that Jesus lived during his life, and the reality he created at his death.

As tragic as it is to imagine, this cross is not the remnants of a failure. It is the evidence of a change so great it destroyed the curtain that all though indestructible. It shattered stones and traditions. It shook the earth and shook the belief that some people are more holy and valuable than other people (Matthew 27:51). This cross — the power of this piece of wood, this cross, that was used by one group of people to make another group of people suffer so much, that power was destroyed by one flogged, robed, crowned, and crucified man.

No more division.

No more.

Amen.

1 Corinthians 15:1-11

I Want To Remind You — Easter Sunday

We have heard it before, but let's hear the story again.

The law of Moses said that if a person was killed by hanging on a tree, their body must not be left there overnight but must be buried before sundown. The Romans in charge of the crucifixion did not care at all about what Moses said, and usually left the bodies hanging there for the animals to remove. That set the best example for people walking past to understand what happened to criminals against Rome. But, maybe it was Joseph of Arimathea, an important member of the Jewish Sanhedrin, who convinced the soldiers to let them take Jesus' body from the cross and move it to one of the tombs that Joseph's family owned. Now, the soldiers wouldn't have cared anymore about the Sanhedrin than they did about Moses, but maybe they saw this as a way to calm things down a bit before it created problems for them in Rome. Anytime a local problem like this got big enough for Caesar to hear about, his solution was to find someone there to blame and make an example of them. So, maybe the guards just wanted to avoid becoming that example and they let them take Jesus' body off of the cross to quiet things down a bit.

They put Jesus' body in the tomb, but then they had another problem. According to the laws of Moses, there were steps they had to take to properly prepare the body for burial. But it was Friday and sundown was the beginning of the sabbath day, and work like burial preparations could not be done on the sabbath. They just had enough time to wrap the body in a clean sheet and planned to return after the sabbath to finish the other steps.

Early on that Sunday morning, they made the trip back to the tomb to finish the burial preparations. Mary got to the quarry first and walked passed the column where the other criminals still hung on their crosses. Then she saw the tomb. The stone door had been opened. The guards were gone. Her heart must have sunk as she wondered if the guards had decided that giving them Jesus' body was not such a good idea and had now taken it to be dumped somewhere else. She stepped inside and saw the body was indeed gone. She sat and wept. That's when it happened.

When the others arrived at the tomb, they not only did not complete the burial preparation the law of Moses required, but they realized that all of those old laws were finally, once and for all, finished. Those laws that said if you violated God's law, you would die. There they stood in the grave of a man who had been called a violator of those laws, was made dead, and was now alive. Jesus had told them there was something more important than the old laws and traditions, and now he proved it.

The tomb was empty. Jesus was risen.

As they walked out of the tomb, they realized that everything they had known and been before had just changed. They understood that from now on, life was not based on things that divided them, but on the one thing that made them all equal members of one group. They were believers in Jesus Christ. God had given them something completely new.

It lasted a few hours at best.

As the day went on and Mary told others about Jesus appearing and talking with her, others began saying they had seen him too. Some said they had not only seen Jesus, but he let them touch him. One group said they had seen him when they were walking down the road, and he not only talked with them but went with them and sat down and ate with them. They all celebrated what they heard, but some of them began wondering. They wondered things like which of them Jesus had appeared to first. They began to wonder what it meant that some had just seen Jesus, others had actually touched him, and still others had even sat at the same table and eaten with him. Did that mean that Jesus thought some of them were more important than others? Did it mean that, although they all believed that God had raised Jesus from the dead, God looked at some of them differently than the others, and maybe some of them were a bit more important than the others? They began to get distracted.

I realize the stories we have about the resurrection don't tell us whether the disciples thought these things then. But, as we look at what was happening in the church as Paul wrote to them just a few decades later, it is clear that those folks had forgotten the fact that they were one, united group who believed in Jesus Christ. They still preached about the empty tomb, but they had forgotten a big part of what it meant that it was empty. And the more they talked and preached about the empty tomb, the more distracted from that message they got.

As Paul wrote his letters, most churches still preached about the empty tomb and celebrated the fact that it promised a new life to those who followed Jesus. But some of them had questions about what it actually meant to follow him. Everyone might get that new life if they believed in Jesus, but what happens if some of those people who believed don't actually live their lives the way we believe someone following Jesus would live? Is the guarantee of equality revocable? Can a member of our unified group of believers be un-unified if we decide they no longer fit? If so, what are the things someone will do, and not do, to live the life a true believer in Jesus would live? And how many votes does it take to un-unify them from the group? Can we still associate with someone who is un-unified from our group? Yes, the tomb was empty and promised new life for all who believed; as long as they truly believed.

What about people who are accepted as true believers in the church in Phillippi? After all, those people don't even require new members to be circumcised. What if a member of the Phillippi church comes here? We believe that following Jesus means being circumcised, so is that visitor a believer or not? And what about those churches in Macedonia? They talk so much about loving each other they even let women speak. What if one of those people comes here and wants to worship with us?

What about the churches in Galatia and those in countries that don't even have the same laws that we have. I mean, you know how they think about marriage, and their other laws let them get away with things we would never allow here. What if one someone from one of those churches came here and wanted to worship with us? Can they? Or do we maybe let them come in, but not let them fully take part? I mean, after all, we believe that Jesus was risen to save everyone, but we have to draw the line somewhere.

Whenever the thinking started, Paul wrote his letters to a church that had gotten distracted. On this day that we remember and celebrate the empty tomb, I wonder if we might agree that we are sometimes still distracted from the message this day announced? For just a few moments, let me see if I can help us create a picture of that Sunday morning that might help us remember what this morning is really about, and might help us keep from becoming quite so distracted.

In your imagination, I invite you to picture that morning. It might help to think about a stone quarry you may have seen some time, or just a big hole dug into down into the ground. It's about the size of half a football field and deep enough to stick a house into. The sides of the quarry are bare rock and have little caves dug into them. If you look inside one of the caves, you'll see it actually has several little rooms carved out of the rock inside. These are tombs. The first room has a big stone along one wall where the body is placed and prepared for burial, and sometime later the body is moved into one of the other rooms alongside the others already there. The caves are dark except for the candles and oil lamps we are carrying. The floor is marked with the drops of wax and oil from the candles and lamps of those who have been here before us. The air is dry and is filled with the smells of incense and the scented oils used in the burial preparations. Can you see it?

But what I really want you to see is outside the cave, in the space outside the tomb. Mary and the others have all gone, so we are the only ones here. We are standing in the center of the quarry looking at the cave where Jesus' body had been placed. The big flat and round stone used as a door is moved and the entrance to the cave is wide open. I really want us to focus on is what we do not see this morning. There, between where we stand and the door to the empty tomb, do you notice?

There are no fences, no lines, nothing at all to separate us from the door. There is nothing to separate anyone from that door. And there are no lines to stand in to divide us up into different groups.

There are no signs listing the rules and requirements defining those who will be allowed to come to the tomb. There are no people walking around carrying clipboards to make sure we are each on the approved list and allowed to be there. No one is handing out passes to allow some of us to enter the tomb first.

Can you see it? There is us, and there is the empty tomb.

That is the image I want to remember on this Easter Sunday. Yes, there is that empty cave and the stories of what happened next. But I want to remember the scene outside that tomb. I want that image to come into my mind this week every time something starts to distract me from Easter morning. When I see someone I disagree with or that doesn't fit some ideas I have created for what it means to be welcomed. I want this image to appear anytime I hear myself mumble about someone I had defined as hopeless or a waste of carbon or someone I will go out of my way to avoid spending any time. I want that image to come into my mind anytime I hear someone try and close the doors to my church, or even roll that rock over a little-bitty-bit to limit anyone being able to step inside.

As someone trying my best to represent the risen Jesus Christ as his ambassador in today's world, that is the Easter morning I want to remember. I want to remember it so I can be reminded that my job is to spend my time announcing that the tomb is empty, and not getting distracted by trying to protect the tomb from having the wrong people come inside.

Let us go now, and spread the good news. Christ is risen! Christ is risen for all.

Amen.

1 John 1:1-2:2

This Little Light Of Mine

Do you remember the story I told you a few weeks ago during Lent about Hap? Hap was a guy who studied his Bible. He read it over and over, underlining, and memorizing. He wasn't just studying, he was searching. He was searching for things he could ask preachers that he was sure they wouldn't know anything about. He made a list of questions like, "What kind of snake gave Eve the apple?" He made his list of questions and then got on his bicycle and rode around town hunting for preachers. When he caught one, and they couldn't answer his question from the scripture, he considered it evidence that they were phonies, and didn't hesitate to say so. "And you call yourself a preacher!" he would say. "It's right there in the book!" he would announce. Sometimes, when he was in one of his moods, he would reach into the basket of his bicycle and pull out the old flashlight he carried there. He would wave it in front of the preacher and say, "God is light, and in him is no darkness at all, preacher. It sounds like your light might some new batteries," and then pedal off in search of the next victim.

By the way, for those wondering about Hap's question about what kind of snake gave Eve the apple, he also spent a lot of time at the library studying the encyclopedia where he read that the most intelligent of all snakes was the king cobra. Since Genesis said that the serpent that met Eve was more crafty than any of the other animals God created, it had to have been a king cobra. As Hap would say, "It's right there in the book!"

One day a friend of Hap's was working on something and asked if he could borrow Hap's flashlight for a minute. Hap said it wouldn't do him any good; there weren't any batteries in it and the bulb was burned-out. He said he didn't carry it for that kind of light. Now, Hap may have been ornery, and maybe not the best example of what studying the Bible is really all about, but it turns out that he actually was a pretty good theologian as we look at our scripture for today, it seems that Hap understood something important about light that we sometimes overlook.

This letter from John was probably written sometime around the year one hundred, probably still before John's gospel was written. So it was one of the early things written to help the young church understand what was expected of them. The church hadn't been around for all that long, but it was already having some serious problems shining its light into the world. That's how John started the letter. He wrote that God is light, and wherever God is, the darkness is taken away (1 John 1:5-6). Everyone understood that when John talked about light he wasn't just talking about things like candles, or oil lamps, or flashlights. The light that God brought was an honest way of behaving, a godlike way of living. Everyone understood that thieves and criminals did their stuff in the dark where they could not be seen, so talking about darkness meant behaving in a way that was not honest, and living a life that was not godlike. The people of the church were to walk in the light.

It was a great analogy because everyone understood that light and darkness cannot exist together. If it is dark and you bring in a light, the darkness goes away. If it is light and you take it away, it gets dark again. It is either light or dark, honest and godlike or dishonest and not godlike. John reminded them that the role of the church and its members was to live in a way that showed they walked in the light. He wrote that if the church said they followed Christ but the people lived their lives like they were walking in darkness, they were liars (1 John 1:7-10).

They all understood that they needed to walk in the light, but they didn't agree on just what that light was, and they weren't all that clear about how you walked in it. There were a lot of opinions, and that led to a lot of disagreements. They looked for someone to help them understand and ended up having a lot of different teachers giving them answers. Some listened to one teacher, some listened to another, and that led to the people of the church beginning to divide themselves up into different, new churches. They all believed they needed to walk in

God's light, but they didn't agree on how to do that.

Today is the Sunday after Easter and we are beginning a new season in the church called Eastertide. Eastertide lasts for fifty days, from Easter Sunday to Pentecost, and throughout history this has been a time when Christians have tried to better understand what Jesus' resurrection really meant to them and to the world. They knew things had changed, but sometimes had a difficult time figuring out what all of the changes really were. Today's passage from John's letter seems to be a good start to our own season of Eastertide.

As I was thinking about all of this, I sat down and did some research. I was curious about a couple of things. First, I wondered just how many different churches we have divided ourselves into today, after all these years. People argue about this too, but most seem to agree that there are something like forty thousand different types of Christian churches in the world today. But, not all of them are there because they split from some other church and don't agree on what walking in the light means. A better way of thinking about is that there are probably just forty real divisions that exist in all of those Christian churches today. Forty different groups of people who agree that we need to walk in God's light, but do not agree on what that light is - from one to forty.

I was curious about the teachers who were helping all of those churches better understand what God's light was all about. It wasn't scientific, but I did a quick search for books that were written to teach what it means to "be Christian." When I got to ten thousand different books explaining what it meant to walk in the light, I quit counting.

I want to be clear, I am not saying that I believe it is wrong for the church to be divided into forty different groups, or that it is wrong that we have so many denominations. I am not saying that I understand the one, true answer to what it means to walk in the light and that we are somehow walking along a brighter path than anyone else.

But I do want to tell you something I heard from John's letter, and from Hap. John reminded me about God's light, but Hap is the one who really kind of woke me up to something I think is important.

It is true that light and dark are opposites and you either have one or the other. It is also true that it is important for us to live our lives in a way that shows we walk in God's light. But, I don't think it is all that important that we all agree on the specific rules for walking in that light. I think God understands that we are all different people, with different backgrounds, living very different lives in very different places. Last week was Easter, when God shined the light into the world in a new way, and I am not concerned about there being forty different paths that Christians believe they should be walking down to be in that light. I may not agree with them, but I believe that God will be able to take care of all forty of our groups without me getting all riled up about it.

John and Hap taught me to not to be so worried about defining how to live my life in a way that shines God's light into the darkness, but to understand *why* I want to shine that light.

There are two choices. Only one of them shows what God's love is all about.

John wrote about living in God's light to show other people where salvation was, so they could use our light as a beacon to find their way out of their darkness and join us in a new life. John calls us to shine our light to help others.

Hap used the light as a weapon. It was something to briefly shine into the darkness so he could point out the weaknesses of others and leave them sitting in their darkness as he rode away. Hap calls us to shine our light to make sure those in the dark know they were in the dark.

Whatever your rules are for how we are supposed to live a life in God's light, ask yourself this question: Am I doing that to catch someone living in the dark, or am I doing it to help remove that darkness?

One way laughs into the darkness and walks away, the other reaches out into the darkness and says, "Here, take my hand."

Only one shows the love that is the message of the resurrection.

And that, my friends, regardless of anything else that may divide us, that is what it means to be one who walks in the light following Jesus Christ.

Amen.

1 John 3:1-7

Righteous, Dude!

The pastor was tired. As he walked into the church for his nine o'clock meeting, he was more like exhausted, not just tired. He hadn't gotten home until after three and wasn't able to get to sleep until almost five because he couldn't stop thinking about it all. He had gotten the call to come to the hospital late yesterday afternoon because there had been an accident. When he got there he learned that it was a horrendous accident, and it involved a young child from his church. She had just sat beside him during the children's sermon that morning, and now he stood beside her in the emergency room. The doctor told him that she would most likely not survive. The doctor was crying, as well as the nurses. They all knew the girl and her family. Two were even neighbors who had an ongoing friendly competition around decorating their yards for Christmas.

As the pastor walked to the waiting room to be with the girl's parents, he realized he needed help. He thought about the girl, her parents, her little brother, the nurses, the doctor, and stopped at the phone to call someone from his church. He explained what had happened, and ten minutes later, three church members arrived at the hospital. They were part of a group at the church who had learned how to just be there at a time like this, and that's what they did for the next many hours. They were there with the family as the doctors tried to save the girl. They were there with the doctor and nurses as they did everything they could do. They were there when the doctor and nurses came to the room to tell the family it was over. They were there in the emergency room as they all prayed together. The pastor went home with the family and was there as they tried to understand what had happened to their family and as they walked, for the first time, into that now-empty bedroom. Others stayed at the hospital to be there with the doctors and nurses as they tried to understand what had happened. Others went to the grandparents' homes to be there as well.

As the pastor finally crawled into bed, he was feeling two things. First, was the pain of what had been lost that night. But second, was a tremendous feeling of joy at what he had just seen those members of his church do. Some of them had been old, one was still a teenager. Some were wealthy and some were barely getting by. Some had strong opinions, and others had just as strong opinions going the other way. But that night none of that mattered. They had come to that hospital as one, with the one goal of loving those who needed that love. The pastor lay awake with the feeling that tonight, he had seen the church as it was meant to be. He had seen those people doing what he believed Jesus would have done. He had been a pastor for many years, but what he saw tonight amazed him. As he walked into his office and joined that nine o'clock meeting, he was exhausted, but he felt that the church, and he, had been reborn.

A few minutes later the church secretary knocked on the door, apologized for interrupting the meeting, and told the pastor he was needed downstairs. She explained there was a problem and he needed to go quickly. As he walked down the stairs he heard the voices. They reminded him of the voices he heard yesterday when he walked into the hospital. But these voices sounded angry. As he entered the room he saw the voices were coming from members of the committee appointed to redecorate the downstairs women's bathroom. Their faces were red, their fingers were pointing, one was standing in the bathroom doorway with her arms folded in front of her and a snarl on her face.

The snarling woman saw the pastor and said something like, "Well, it's about time!" and demanded that he settle the issue once and for all. When the pastor asked, he learned that the committee members were arguing about which shade of blue would be used to paint the bathroom. They had been arguing about it since getting there an hour ago. They started yelling and finger-pointing again, and the arm-folder stood a bit taller in the doorway. They finally stopped and looked at the pastor.

"Well?" the arm-folder inquired.

The pastor looked at them. Then he turned, walked out of the room, up the stairs, out the door, and got in his car. He didn't to back to the meeting, and he didn't tell his secretary he was leaving. He wouldn't have known where to tell her he was going anyway. He just needed to go. He needed some time.

Some people thought he overreacted, and that he could have just picked a shade of blue and been done with it, or maybe suggest a nice shade of green they might all agree on. After all, that kind of problem-solving was just part of the job of working with people. The secretary thought he was just tired after the long night, and told the committee he probably would come back after a nice nap and solve the problem later, and apologize to the committee for walking out in such a non-pastoral way.

But as he drove around, he wasn't thinking about problem solving and wasn't thinking about going back to talk about paint or to apologize for anything. He was thinking about how quickly things had changed. How quickly it had gone from watching the church stand together and do things that made such a difference in people's lives, to seeing it stand around a basement bathroom door with arms folded, fingers pointing, and voices shouting — about paint.

He felt as if something had been ripped from him. Something that had caused him to feel that the hope had been replaced with more of the same old thing from the past. He wondered which of those was the real church? Was what happened last night too much to expect to last? Was that feeling of being a part of such a powerful, loving community something that might just come and go now and then on those rare occasions? He found himself driving until he was in front of the house of the family who had just lost their daughter. He stopped and went inside. He was there to care for the family… and himself.

As I think about that story, I think about the words John wrote in today's passage. John was writing to people who were arguing about what meant to be the church.

Little children, let no one deceive you. Everyone who does what is right is righteous, just as he is righteous.

(1 John 3:7)

First, let's make sure we're reading what John wrote. When John wrote that people should do what is "right", he wasn't saying they should do what they believed was the correct thing to do based on their opinions. It didn't mean following rules or policies the church may have implemented to maintain order. It had nothing to do with the views or opinions anyone there might have. Doing right meant doing what God had shown was the thing that should be done.

I've taken the time to explain that because of the many times I hear Christians arguing over some issue, each insisting their view is the "right" view. They usually base it on the interpretation of something from the Bible, and the argument is essentially an attempt to prove that their interpretation is the correct one, and their opponent's interpretation is the wrong one. For them, doing the right thing means doing the thing they agree with, the thing they have decided is the right thing to do.

When John wrote that the church should do the right thing, he meant something different. God had established what it meant to do right, not the church. John spent the rest of his letter reminding them about it. I'll try to summarize it for us. In short, it goes like this.

It goes back to that Easter morning message.

God loved us so much that he sent his own son to die and then be resurrected to show that the old laws that had divided us were destroyed. We did not earn it, God gave it to us. The only thing that God asks of us in return is that we love each other as much as we were loved. How much is that? Jesus showed that he loved us so much that he cared more about us than he did his own life. What God did was righteous.

As I read John's words, I think about the things the pastor and church members did that night at the hospital and in the homes. If I wanted to find an example of someone doing something that demonstrated what God considered "right", that would be it. And then I think about the committee standing at the bathroom door. If I wanted to find an example of someone doing something that fell short of God's definition of "right", that would be it.

That is what I believe it means to do the right thing; to do the thing that focuses on the needs of others more than on our own needs. Being righteous means living our lives in a way that shows we care more about others than we do ourselves. We don't have to be "right" as a way to win. We want to do "right" as a way of showing how much we care.

In my mind, I think the difference between the two rights is that one of them means doing something for me and the other means doing something for someone else. One is the act of someone wanting to win something for themselves, the other is the act of someone showing care and compassion to someone else. One argues about paint, the other holds someone's hand. Only one is about God's love.

Amen.

I Love You — If You Know What I Mean

The young couple sat together and they gazed into each other's eyes. One leaned toward the other, but the other hesitated and leaned away. "But, I love you," the first spoke, "C'mon, it's okay; you know I love you."

The parent looked into the child's eyes and said, "You understand that I did that because I love you?" The child held their swollen cheek and tried to nod. "And because I love you so much, it is my responsibility to teach you the difference between right and wrong." The child tried to nod again. "But," the parent said, "some people don't understand what it means to love someone. So if anyone asks, you tell them that bruise came from your ballgame this afternoon; understand?"

The nation that says it is founded on God's love and has almost unlimited material possessions, sometimes puts people who have come to them suffering and possessing nothing, into detention camps, taking children from their parents and putting them in to crowded cages where they are abused and lost in red tape. That nation proclaims they are doing it to teach those people and the world what it means to do the right thing.

The woman who has just buried her child comes to the church to try and find some easing of the pain that is tearing her life apart. The church smiles at her and says, "God loves you so much that he is just testing you and has given you this loss to make you stronger. But don't worry because God will never give you more than you can bear."

We could all give more examples, but let me stop here and ask the obvious question: What does it mean to love someone? We say and hear it a lot: I love you. I imagine many of us have said it a few times today. I love you. Why do we say it? What do we mean when we say it? I guess there are a lot of reasons. Sometimes we say it because we are overwhelmed with feelings for someone dear to us. Sometimes we say it because we want something. Sometimes we say it to justify something we have done or want to do. Sometimes we say it to get out of trouble for something we did, or forgot to do. Sometimes we say it because someone else said it to us first.

I love you.

John wrote today's passage to the early church to help them understand what it meant on Easter morning when God said, "I love you." They understood it meant they were to love others as God loved them, but they had different ideas as to just what that meant.

The couple had been married for several years when the husband had the experience that led him to make the decision to become a Christian and join that church. His wife was not opposed to his decision and was not by any means a bad person, but while she did come to church with her husband, she did not feel the desire to convert to Christianity and become a full member of the church. Out of their love and concern for the husband, a committee from the church went to the husband and urged him to leave his wife because she was a threat to his own salvation. The couple was happily married and their religious differences had no impact at all upon that marriage. But he still divorced his wife and never spoke with her again.

There was a family that had been a part of everyone's lives before the local church was started. They ran a store that everyone in town went to and supported. That family did not join the church when it began, although they continued to do all they could to help and support the entire community. The members of the church no longer shopped in that family's store. They no longer talked with anyone from that family. As a result, the family business was failing and the family was going to lose their home. Church members loved that family enough, they tried to help the family understand that they needed to join the church.

And there was the man who recently moved to town and was staying with family members. He was lonely and afraid after having to leave his home and start over in a new place. He was active in his previous church, and he attended the morning service there with his relatives who are members of this church. The church he used to attend, and still officially belongs to, believes it is acceptable for women to take an active role in their services, which is something this church does not believe. Because the church loves the man so much, as he comes to the altar with his family to take part in communion this morning, he is passed by and not allowed to take part in the Lord's Supper.

John was writing to a church that was trying to understand what it meant to love others the way God wanted them to love. He explained it by writing,

> *We know love by this, that he laid down his life for us — and we ought to lay down our lives for one another. How does God's love abide in anyone who has the world's goods and sees a brother or sister in need and yet refuses to help?*
> *Little children, let us love, not in word or speech, but in truth and action.*

(1 John 3:16-18)

From a couple thousand years away, that one line seems pretty clear,

> *How does God's love abide in anyone who has the world's goods and sees a brother or sister in need and yet refuses to help?*

(1 John 3:17)

It's not one of those vague, theological things like John wrote at the beginning of his gospel. This sounds like something they all should have understood then, and we should understand today. Right?

Nope. Let's look at what the early church did with that statement, and what we tend to still do today.

First, they asked just who this "each other" is that we are to lay our lives down for? In other places, John says "brothers and sisters." Some of those in the church, then and now, take that to mean brothers and sisters in the church; those who believe what we believe. Those who are not a part of our faith? Nah, those aren't included in the command.

For me to love you as God wants me to, first be a part of my group; my church, my country, my race, my social views, my status, my... it's a long list. But I will remind us there were no lines or fences outside the empty tomb on Easter morning and no list of qualifications for being one of those that Jesus died for. In fact, that morning there wasn't even a church to belong to if you wanted. Jesus died for everyone, everywhere, and that is the criteria for those we are to love; be someone, somewhere.

People don't have to somehow earn our love any more than we earned God's love. And to be honest with you, if love was something that we had to earn, I think we would all pretty much be out of luck.

Okay then, I'm supposed to love everyone, everywhere, and when I see someone in need, I am to not just show God's love with words, but with actions. But what kind of actions? What does loving them mean? Weren't the actions of those groups in the church showing God's love by forcing those people to realize they needed to change? Isn't it an act of love to sometimes make a point; isn't that what 'tough love' is all about?

I think John would point out that the idea of 'tough love' is something we created, not God. Receiving God's love was pretty much the opposite of tough. That was it. Loving a brother or sister doesn't mean we are emotionally 'in love' with them. It means we value them as fellow children of God and will help them when they have a need.

But one Bible version of John's passage says we should show pity for the suffering. Isn't showing pity an action?

I think John would say that, if we pity someone who is suffering, it does not mean we feel sorry for them or we are saying "tsk tsk" while we shake our heads at how unfortunate they are and why we believe they are where they are. For John, having pity means we are doing something to help remove the person's suffering. If what we do ignores the suffering, or somehow increases that suffering, or somehow uses that person's suffering as an opportunity to try to teach a lesson or prove something we believe in, whatever it is we are doing is not an act of God's love.

Okay, I am to love everyone, everywhere. When I see someone in need and suffering I am to do something that eases that suffering. But, tell me this, what does it actually mean to be in need? What if that person could probably ease their suffering all on their own if they just tried to work a little harder, or straightened out their behavior? Is that really a need I should be helping with? Wouldn't it be better if I let them fix it themselves? I mean, if I do it and they don't change their ways, what's going to keep them from getting back in the same situation later?

I wonder if John might respond by saying that another person's suffering is not based on our rules or opinions? Whether or not a person is suffering and feeling pain isn't based on what we believe qualifies as legitimate suffering. We just need to remember that each one of us has the same need for some feeling of security, the need for access to food and nourishment, the need to feel that we have a place at the human table of worth, the need to feel at least some small piece of hope. When any of those are missing, we suffer. I don't need to agree with their suffering, I just need to help ease it. I just need to share God's love with them and give them the opportunity to look at the world differently than they do now. It isn't my responsibility to worry about what they will do after I love them. God will take care of that. My job is to love them. If I am spending my time classifying the one in need, I am not acting. That means I am not loving.

The members of the early church John wrote to all believers that they should love their brothers and sisters, but they did not agree on what it meant to love, and who their brothers and sisters were that should be loved. We come here two thousand years later and hear the same words,

How does God's love abide in anyone who has the world's goods and sees a brother or sister in need and yet refuses to help?
(1 John 3:17)

How are we doing? When we see someone in need, especially someone who looks and acts very differently than us, who does not know how to do things the way we do things, who does not believe all of the same things we believe, who maybe came here from a place we aren't familiar with, and who maybe came here in a way that wasn't how people are supposed to come here, what is our response?

How are we doing?

Do we try to understand and accept them as our brother or sister in need? Do we do something to help remove their suffering? Do we do something to try and give them hope?

Do we love our brothers and sisters as God first loved us?

When we say, "I love you," just what do we mean?

Amen.

Fifth Sunday of Easter

1 John 4:7-21

Perfect Love

I want to begin by being very honest with you and admit that I have some very real problems with today's passage from John's letter. It's not that I don't think I understand what John is saying, but I am afraid that I do understand what he is saying. And if my understanding is correct, it is causing me to take a fresh look at who we are, and what we are doing as the church.

It has always been very difficult to be the church in the world. The early church faced all kinds of horrible attacks. Sometimes they came from people in the community who did terrible things to those people in town who belonged to the church. Sometimes entire governments took action against the church, arresting, torturing, and killing those who believed in Jesus Christ. The church has faced attack again and again, not just from groups like the Romans and radicals during the Reformation. At most any point in history we can find the church under persecution someplace in the world, as well as individuals, governments, other religions, and cultures. We frequently hear or read about Christians facing horrific things in China, Russia, North Korea, and many others, simply because they wanted to worship God. It seems there has never been a time the church was not threatened by someone.

But in today's passage, John reminded me that the greatest threat to our being the church may not be one of those. The biggest threat to us being the church we have been called to be might actually be an inside threat; something right in here. It isn't a person or group. It isn't a government or other religious faith. John made me wonder if the truest, greatest threat we face in being the church is something in our minds — a thought or a fear. Not a fear like those faced by those in history in and in different countries today; the fear of being arrested, persecuted, or killed, but a very real fear that lives inside each one of us here that sometimes keeps us from being the church we have been called to be. It is that fear that keeps us from loving others in the way that God commands us to love them.

Last week we talked about God's command that we were to love our brothers and sisters. As far as Easter morning was concerned, anyone who is breathing a living breath is God's child, which makes them our brother or sister. Loving a brother or sister doesn't mean we are emotionally 'in love' with them. It means we value them as fellow children of God and will help them when they have a need. John said when we see a brother or sister in need, we aren't to love them with words safely from a distance, but we are to put their needs before our own and do something to ease their pain. That is what John said it means to love each other and what it means to do God's will, individually and together as the church.

Here is my problem today. If that is what we are to be as Christians and as the church, people who believe that the needs of our brothers and sisters are more important than our own needs, and that we should help them when they suffer, why then do we spend so much time and energy talking and worrying about our own needs and about protecting ourselves from our brothers and sisters?

If our reason for being here is to love our brothers and sisters, why don't we do that?

What do I mean? Look around at what you see and hear. How many times have you heard Christians worrying about their fears instead of how to love? How many times have you heard Christians talk about a social issue or political viewpoint as a threat to the church and to Christianity itself? How many times have you heard Christians talk about a group of people as a threat to the church and Christianity itself?

They are coming for us, they say. They hate us and want to destroy us, they say. They will destroy our marriages and families. They will corrupt our children, they say. We need to change laws to stop them, they say. We need to hold them up for ridicule and show them as the unbelievers they really are, they say. We need to find a way to remove them from here, they say. We must do whatever it takes to protect the church and the Christian faith from them, they say — from them — from our brothers and sisters.

I'll ask again. If our reason for being here is to love our brothers and sisters, why don't we do that?

Especially when we hear John say that anyone who says they love God but hates a brother or sister is a liar. I don't know about you, but where I grew up you if you were arguing with someone you could call them pretty much any name in the book. Call them a fool, or an idiot, but if you ever called them a liar you had crossed the line. I have a difficult time thinking that any of us want to be thought of as a liar. Why is it, then, that we claim to love God, when if we are honest with ourselves, we know there are some of our brothers and sisters that we simply do not love enough to go and ease their suffering?

If loving our brother and sister means believing that their needs are more important than our own needs, aren't we making ourselves pretty vulnerable by doing that?

John wrote,

There is no fear in love. But perfect love drives out fear....

(1 John 4:18 NIV)

As I think about John's words, I think I see a few of the ways our fear is getting in the way of us focusing on loving our brothers and sisters.

First, is the idea that we need to fear those brothers and sisters who do not share our faith and we believe are trying to destroy the church and the Christian faith with their legal actions or their lifestyles. Pick a topic and we'll find churches and groups making this the center of everything they do. Their message is about enemies that exist, about the dangers that need to be feared and battled. They talk about how they believe someone must act to remain pure and faithful in this dangerous age.

To those people, I offer my love and say that I believe God is powerful enough to protect the church and the faith. I respect your enthusiasm, but we were not called to be God's security force. We were called to love our brothers and sisters. Yes, they believe different things, some of which we strongly disagree with, but they are not enemies. There have always been issues that have challenged the church, yet the church stands here today. No ideas are powerful enough to be a threat to God.

If we can identify a perceived threat and make it big enough that a lot of people are going to see it as a threat to them personally, it is a powerful way to pull people together and build a group or any movement like a church. Having a common enemy is a wonderful motivator and will cause people to blindly follow anyone who offers the answer to that fear. But that is not the way we have been commanded to be the church. No, our role as the church is not to identify and spend our time trying to defend ourselves from those we call enemies. Our role is to love all people enough to remove those fears rather than feed them. There are no enemies; there are only brothers and sisters.

There is a fear in our minds that I believe is even more dangerous to us. It is a rather strange one. It is the idea that, if we really do what we are called to do and preach about loving our brothers and sisters, no one will come. After all, let's be honest, there are some people who absolutely do not want to love some other people. They are not about to come to a church that constantly reminds them exactly what they should be doing. We find other things to talk about to make the church feel a bit more welcoming — to make it sound easier.

We spend our time talking about how God wants us all to be happy and wants us to be successful, and perhaps even wants us to be wealthy. We talk about the ways that our faith can make our lives easier and happier. We talk about ways our faith can take away the risks and dangers of normal life. We design comfortable and successful looking places to worship and offer a wide range of ways to worship to see that everyone can worship in a way that fits their comfort level. We do those things because they seem to work, and it is important for us to keep growing as a church.

To those people I offer my love and say that I respect their creative attempts to relate to people, but we were not called to create carefully designed and decorated places where we go sit in front of stages to hear presentations about God, but to gather in places where the focus was on those of us in the pews and what we bring to offer to the one we remember on the cross at the front of the room. I am not opposed to strategies for church growth, or large, nice church buildings and sanctuaries. But we must not be confused and allow our fears to keep us from being the church that offers the true message that Jesus never promised happiness, success, wealth, or that following him would make our lives easier, happier, and take away the risks. He promised us that following him would make life harder, bring unhappiness, failure, the giving up of wealth, and we would face risk after risk along the way. Being a church that says our one command is to love our brothers and sisters may not fill the pews, but it is the message we have been called to share.

To tell the truth, in my experience, those churches who were able to overcome their fears and demonstrate what it meant to share God's love did just fine.

There is one other way I believe that fear can get in the way of our loving others. Sometimes we do not love simply because we are afraid of getting hurt. Let's be honest. Love is a risky and dangerous thing. Some of us have been hurt by love and that was by people we thought we knew and understood. Now we're supposed to love people we don't know, or that are very, very different than we are? That is scary.

But that is what we are called to do: to love our brothers and sisters — all of them.

Not just those in my group or who live nearby, or come from my country. Not just those who believe exactly what I believe. Not just those who speak my language, dress like me or eat the foods I eat. Not just those who have the kind of background I have or live the lifestyle I believe they should live.

Yes, that sometimes makes it terrifying, which is why John wrote that perfect love drives out fear.

What is perfect love? I'll tell you what I think it is.

I see perfect love each time I see you reach out together to comfort someone who is hurting. I see perfect love each time I see you gather gifts or supplies to send to someone who has a need. I see perfect love each time I see you carry a meal to someone, or offer a ride, or sit by their bedside, or call on the phone, or send that email. I see perfect love each time you dare to take the risk and join together to do what we have been told to do; to love our brother and sisters as God first loved us.

Amen.

Sixth Sunday of Easter

1 John 5:1-6

It Takes Both

Ellen hadn't said a word since the Bible study began a half-hour earlier. No one thought anything about it since it was the first time she had attended the meetings. Plus, she was just home for Christmas from her first year of college, so she was much younger than the rest of the group. There were eight other adults in the group and the pastor. But the most vocal member was Frank. Frank was nearing seventy and was not at all shy about speaking up when he had something to say, which was most of the time. Frank had very strong feelings about the Bible, and this study on the book of Acts gave him lots of opportunities to present them. At one point near the end of the hour, Frank made a comment about something and the pastor heard Ellen mumble. He asked if she wanted to share something or if she had a question. Ellen hesitated, looked down at the floor, then sat up in her seat and looked straight at the pastor.

"Why didn't you tell us about this?" she said. "I grew up in this church and went every Sunday but no one ever talked about it. Why didn't you teach us about this?"

The look on her face caught the pastor, and everyone else, by surprise. It wasn't curiosity, but anger.

"Teach what?" the pastor asked, "I don't understand."

"I think you did it on purpose because you are afraid if we knew the truth, things might happen you couldn't control. That's why, isn't it? You're afraid."

Everyone looked at Ellen and then at the pastor.

"I honestly don't know what you are talking about, Ellen," he said calmly, "what do you think I didn't tell you about?"

"The spirit!" Ellen almost shouted. "The Holy Spirit. Why didn't you tell us about the Holy Spirit giving us the power to do things like interpret the scriptures and have the other powers? I came here every week and never once heard anyone tell me about what God really is about, and what we can do because of the Holy Spirit. Why didn't you tell me?"

It was Frank who spoke next. "I suppose you mean other things we can do like speaking in tongues and things like that?" He said it with a slight smile that an older man might offer to a teenager who was still naïve and needing his help.

"Yes!" she said. "And the fact that if we believe in the Holy Spirit, it gives us the ability to work other wonders and miracles. We never…"

"That's not what the Bible says that God sent the Holy Spirit for", Frank said. "And if you study the other…"

"And tonight," Ellen said as she looked directly into Frank's eyes. "We've been here an hour with the book of Acts that teaches all about what the Holy Spirit can offer us, and all you've done is talk about what other people have said about it. You don't need to study those people. All of our studying isn't going to help us. The Holy Spirit gives the ability to truly understand the word of God to those who accept him. That's how we understand God's word. I don't think any of you have ever really accepted the Holy Spirit, have you?"

The pastor took a breath and tried. "Ellen, I think I understand what you are saying, and I do understand. Some churches put more emphasis on the Holy Spirit, while others put more emphasis on other parts of the Bible they believe are most important. Our church is one of those that…"

"That doesn't believe in the Holy Spirit and what the Bible really says!" Ellen said as she stood, picked up her coat, and walked out of the room.

Does that sound dramatic? For some, it may also sound familiar, but it isn't new. The group of people I just described were involved in an argument that began among the members of the church John was writing to two thousand years ago.

We know that as the early church grew, people came to the faith from different backgrounds and philosophies. Some of the newcomers were not willing to give up those old views of the world when they converted. In the church John wrote to, there were two key groups that had held on to their previous beliefs and were trying to use them to redefine their new faith in Jesus Christ. One of those we call gnosticism and the other we call docetism.

We'll avoid sounding like a seminary class with a detailed theological explanation. I'll just say that both of those groups believed in Jesus, but who they believed Jesus actually was, was very different. According to the tradition that started the church, Jesus was the Son of God born from a virgin, and the Holy Spirit formally announced his true identity at his baptism. Although he was God's Son, he lived his life as a human, even to the point of dying on the cross before God raised him from the dead. Because of that, salvation was an unearned gift from God who loved us, and the role of the church is to pass that love along to everyone else.

But the two new groups of people coming into the church had other ideas. One group, the Gnostics believed that Jesus was not fully human. He was conceived and born just like any other human, and at his baptism the Holy Spirit came to him to guide his ministry. When Jesus was crucified, before he died, the Holy Spirit left him on the cross and returned to God. They did not believe that God truly became human, and the true presence of God in the story is the presence of the Holy Spirit that came, left, and then came again. And it is that Holy Spirit that is the real key, not some part-God, part-human being. The Spirit provides what we need not any human effort or understanding. The Spirit teaches us what we need to know, we do not find it through our own, human questioning and study.

The other group also believed that Jesus was someone different from the story the church told. This group believed that God was a part of a massive spiritual realm made up of hundreds of heavens that included many levels of holy beings. They did not believe that the reason people were in need of salvation was not because of something God did, but because of an error made by another heavenly being by the name of Sophia, or Wisdom. Because of that, salvation that was not something needed to be back in God's favor. Salvation was the goal of humans to learn and understand enough to gain enough wisdom to correct Sophia's error and earn our place back in the heavenly realm. Jesus was God's presence on earth to teach us that wisdom and to guide us on our way as we continued to learn and earn our own salvation.

Sound confusing? What it means is that there were two groups trying to change what the church believed and preached. One group said that all human effort was useless and the key to our salvation came from God's Holy Spirit that came with the water at Jesus' baptism. The other said that it was the spirit world that had created the problems in the first place, and the key to our salvation was the blood of Jesus that showed he was fully human, and that our human efforts to learn and understand are what will earn us back our place in the heavens.

That is why John wrote to the church,

*Who is it that conquers the world but the one who believes that
Jesus is the Son of God?
This is the one who came by water and blood, Jesus Christ, not
with the water only but with the water and the blood. And the Spirit
is the one who testifies, for the Spirit is the truth.*

(1 John 5:5-6)

The church believed it was both water and blood that made the difference. Jesus was fully man, and fully God, not something in-between. God loved us so much he came to earth and faced our ultimate opponent, death itself, and defeated it.

You may be asking what in the world this might have to say to us today. We don't hear many people running around claiming to be gnostics or docetists, so what does it matter? While we don't usually use terms like gnostics and docetists, we all know that the arguments these two groups made are still very much alive. One insists that the salvation the church offers comes to those who accept the role of the spirit and follow its lead. The other insists that we must think for ourselves, ask questions, and try to understand what we must do for salvation.

What we need to realize about both of these either/or approaches is that they stand directly in the way of the message we heard on Easter morning; that message that we have been given a new beginning without the divisions and the pain they bring. Either way, the message is gone.

The argument that we must set aside our humanity and unquestionably accept the direction of a Holy Spirit only means we run the risk of dividing ourselves into groups who each follow the person who they believe is the truest believer and the better, more correct interpreter of that spirit.

The argument that insists we must set aside any spiritual involvement and rely fully upon our human efforts to learn and understand, means we run the risk of being divided into groups who gather around the teacher they believe has the most correct understanding or who believes those who learn the most information and memorize more lines are closer to God than others.

We can see those divisions in the church today as people like Frank consider any mention of God's Spirit as being foolishness, and others like Ellen consider anyone who questions that group's interpretation of the Holy Spirit's teaching to be a lack of true faith.

These either/or beliefs cause us to look at each other not as brothers and sisters but as opposing forces. You follow, or you are not with us. We are divided. That is not the message we received standing in that stone quarry on Easter morning.

It took water and blood. Human and divine. Together on Easter morning, they destroyed the philosophies and laws that created and enforced divisions between us. Those divisions that claimed that some of us are more holy than others, more correct than others, more valuable than others; those divisions were destroyed by the water and the blood. Anything that attempts to recreate those divisions, anything at all, distracts from our one responsibility of loving our brothers and our sisters.

Amen.

Ephesians 1:15-23

Thank You!

I have something interesting for you to try. It's something you can do as you go through the day, or even when you are stuck in a line somewhere like the grocery store. I thought of it the other day after I read today's passage Paul wrote to the people in Ephesus. Paul was telling them how thankful he was for what they had been doing. At first, it just seemed like one of those passages we skim over as we look for the good stuff. But as I read it again and tried to understand what he was saying, I started thinking about all of the different ways we all have of saying "thank you" and that's when I got the idea.

Just for fun, I spent the next day paying attention to how people thanked other people. There was the guy at the gas station coming out the door in his suit and talking into air to that phone in his ear. As the teenage skateboarder held the door open for him, the man walked past, stopped, looked back, reached out his hand and gave the boarder a thumbs up and a smile. The kid holding the door returned a "No prob, dude!"

Inside the station, the woman was trying to balance the infant on her hip while calming her toddler who was crying after spilling her giant slurpy on the floor. The elderly woman walked over with a stack of napkins and started mopping up the mess, at one point handing a napkin to the toddler who smiled like a big girl and started helping clean the mess. The mother whispered the words "thank you" but her eyes showed how much those words actually meant.

There was the man with the one bag who simply nodded briefly when the person with the full grocery cart told him to go ahead in the line. There was the young boy who smiled but had to be reminded what to say when he was offered the piece of candy. There was the man on his phone saying "thank you" to the nurse from the doctor's office who had called to tell him the tests had come back just fine. There was the "yeah, thanks" from the girl who had just been offered a refill of her iced tea at the restaurant. There was the man lying in the bed who tried to whisper "thank you" to his wife and the hospice nurse who had just moved his pillows to ease his pain.

Try it sometime. When we look for it, it's kind of amazing how many times we actually do say it in some way as we go through our day. Thank you.

As I took another look at Paul's words, I started wondering what he was really saying to the folks at Ephesus. Was this one of those formal kinds of thank you things, like the one the little boy had to be reminded to give? Or was this more like the encouraging thumbs-up giving to the skateboarder holding the door? Was this something more like some of the others, one of those that came from someplace much deeper? As I looked at the words again, I started to believe this was not Paul just nodding his head at them, and it occurred to me that Paul may be giving me an idea for what I might say to you when I want to say "thank you."

And I do. I want to thank you for giving me the opportunity to be the minister I believe I have been called to be. I want to thank you for accepting me when I may have gotten distracted from that role. I want to thank you for how I see you caring for each other, and how you respond when one of us experiences difficult times. I want to thank you for how you care for others who are not here with us and may not be like us in other ways. I want to thank you for being who you are, and for being this church in this community. Thank you.

I want to use Paul's words to try and explain my prayers for you; what I pray you will find as we continue our time together.

I pray that God will give you the wisdom to find the answers to all of the questions you face each day. Am I doing the right thing? Am I really making a difference? What is really important in my life? I pray that God gives you the understanding to answer all of the questions that might be living in your mind so someday you will know without a doubt that you are being the person God has created you to be.

I pray that God will open your eyes and your hearts to see the full truth of the hope and riches that God has given to you. The hope and riches that can't be taken from you now, that is not measured, counted, and divided into percentage levels of who has the most. It is the hope and riches that come from knowing you are God's child, created to be something unique in the world and of equal value with all of your brothers and sisters. I pray that you understand that is your inheritance as a child of God. It is not something you need to struggle and search for, but something that has already been given to you, just waiting for you to see it.

I pray that God gives you the wisdom to understand the great amount of power you have been given as a part of this community right here, this church. While we all sometimes become distracted, I pray God will always remind you of what we can truly accomplish here when we remember who we are. I pray God will always remind you of what we can accomplish when we join our hands together to do God's work. I pray God will always remind you how many pains we can heal when we join our hearts and care for those around us. I pray God will always remind you of how many broken relationships we can mend; how many broken hearts, dreams, and broken lives we can mend when we look at each other as equal brothers and sisters and plow down the things that try to separate us into us and them.

At first glance, Pauls' words today looked to me to be something to skim through as I looked for the good stuff. Come to find out, those words were the good stuff.

To Paul, and to you, I say "thank you." I pray that God will give you the understanding of how to say "thank you" to those who add something to your life.

Amen.

The Big One

I believe it would be safe for me to say that we live in a very divided world. It isn't anything new; pick any period in history and we'll find a world divided by beliefs. Although I believe we can say that, today, we have many new, powerful, and sometimes dangerous abilities to express those divisions. Unless we hide in a dark room by ourselves, it is impossible to go through a day without being reminded of just how divided we have become. Sometimes, to be honest with you, finding that dark room sounds pretty tempting.

Over the past weeks of Lent and Eastertide, we have been thinking about what it means to be a follower of Jesus Christ and to be a part of the church in this divided world. We keep coming back to that stone quarry and the empty tomb inside. We keep coming back to the reality that there were no requirements for coming to that empty tomb, and no restrictions to keep anyone away. We keep coming back to understanding that Jesus was the Son of God and lived as one of us. He did things that went against the laws created by the people in power and they killed him because of it. That was the power of their law. You obey, conform, be like us, or you die.

Then, on Easter morning, the tomb was empty.

The power of the laws that divided us was gone. The Son of God had thrown those old laws away, along with the divisions they created. God didn't do it because we deserved it. God did it because we are loved — all of us — no divisions. No law-followers and law-breakers, no us and no them — we are all loved. We keep coming back to the understanding that Jesus lived and died to give us a new life in which all of us matter. We keep coming back to the understanding that our role as followers of Jesus Christ and as the church is to live our lives the same way he lived his: to love our brothers and sisters and when we see one of them in need, we do something to ease that need.

No more divisions.

We read the line from today's scripture,

Whoever has the Son has life; whoever does not have the Son of God does not have life.

(1 John 5:12)

We are reminded of the words John wrote in his gospel when Jesus said he was the way, the truth, and the life, and that no one came to the Father but through him (John 14:6). It is difficult to hear these words without drawing a line somewhere and dividing people up. On one side are those who are in, and on the other side are those who are out. It is a pretty clear division.

This week is the final week of Eastertide, the time we spend after Easter trying to understand what it means to be the church. Next week is Pentecost, the day we remember the Holy Spirit arriving to give the church the power to get out there and be what it is supposed to be. So, after all we have thought about, just what is it that we are to be? If our role as ambassadors of Christ is to remove divisions, what do we do about John writing that a division exists?

Some followers and some churches see John's words as the central point of what they are to be and do. There is a division. Some are in and some are out, and our role is to make sure we are on the "in" side of the dividing line. We do that by following God's word and keeping ourselves apart from, and protected from, those on the other side. They are lost and we are found and we want to make sure we stay found.

Others see the division, but they understand their role is to go out and find those on the wrong side of the dividing line and do whatever they can to convince those lost ones to come over to their side. They are lost and we are found and our role is to save as many of them as we can.

There are others who see the division but spend their time trying to explain John's words in a way that recognizes them as scripture, yet doesn't require them to divide people up like that. Some of these folks point out that John is the only one who wrote about Jesus saying these things. While the other gospel writers told us what Jesus said as he lived, they didn't record him making this statement. These people suggest that when John wrote those words, he had something specific in mind and wasn't trying to create some absolute division for the entire world. Paul and the other letter writers did that, so maybe that's what John was doing. They point out that when John wrote, there were a lot of other people and groups claiming to offer an easier path to God. And they say that John may have been writing specifically about those others to say that compared to them, Jesus was the only true way to God.

Others don't debate why John wrote the words, but try to understand what John actually meant when he said someone "has the Son." If someone "has the Son" does that mean they say they believe in Jesus, or that they joined a specific group, or does it mean that they live their lives in the same way that Jesus would live his? They wonder if maybe those people we think are on the other side of the divider actually do "have the Son," but in a way that is different from the way we do.

Still other followers and churches see the division in John's words and just do their best to pretend it isn't there. They talk about other things and try to ignore what John said, hoping no one asks about it.

Just what do we do with those words? What does it mean to be a follower of Jesus Christ? What does it mean to be the church? What am I supposed to do?

To be honest with you, no matter what answer I might offer you today, someone is going to be upset about it. The reality is that we are divided, not just in the world outside of the church, but within the church as well. Some believe there is a very clear line between those who are with God and those who are not with God, and what makes the difference is whether or not you say you believe in Jesus as the Christ. Others believe that it is not enough to say you believe, but you must show evidence of your belief by living your life in a certain way, regardless of who you say you follow. And there are others, yet. No matter what answer we might offer to the questions, someone will disagree.

All I can do is try to remember that stone quarry that where the things originally happened that John and the others would write about later. That quarry where Jesus was killed and buried because he was on the wrong side of a dividing line created by rules and laws. That quarry where a big rock was used to seal his tomb and where, armed, Roman Centurions stood outside to enforce the laws and make sure nothing happened. That quarry where, even with the rock and the Centurions outside, God made something happen.

All I can do is try to remember that when they came to the quarry and found that tomb empty, there was nothing else there to divide them up or limit who could be there. There was no notice on a signboard saying that this resurrection was brought to you by God for all of those on this side of the line.

Jesus lived his life stepping over any divisions, and doing what he could do to remove those divisions. I believe if I want to live my life as Jesus would live it, I have no choice but to do the same. If I spend my time focusing on divisions, even those from words like John's, I believe I am being distracted from the life Jesus would live.

Mine is not necessarily the one, correct answer. Mine is not the answer that many others will agree with. Some will believe my answer is misguided, and simply shows that I am not a true believer. My answer is not me saying that I am right, and the answers given by those other groups are wrong.

But my answer is the one I believe I am being called to give. We are called to be ambassadors for Christ. He lived his life looking for brothers and sisters in need and then doing something to ease that need. All brothers and sisters. Every last one of them.

I can do no other.

Amen.

www.ingramcontent.com/pod-product-compliance
Lightning Source LLC
Chambersburg PA
CBHW032022090426
42741CB00006B/706